Secrets of the OLD BILOXI CEMETERY

Secrets of the
OLD BILOXI CEMETERY

John Cuevas

Contributions by Nick Black; Photography by Jason Taylor and Chris Cahill

The History Press

Published by The History Press
Charleston, SC
www.historypress.com

First published 2021

Manufactured in the United States

ISBN 9781467150156

Library of Congress Control Number: 2021937139

Notice: The information in this book is true and complete to the best of our knowledge. It is offered without guarantee on the part of the author or The History Press. The author and The History Press disclaim all liability in connection with the use of this book.

Do not stand at my grave and weep. I am not there. I do not sleep. I am a thousand winds that blow. I am the diamond glints on snow. I am the sunlight on ripened grain. I am the gentle autumn rain. When you awaken in the morning's hush, I am the swift uplifting rush of quiet birds in circling flight. I am the soft star that shines at night. Do not stand at my grave and cry. I am not there. I did not die.

—Elizabeth Lucas

CONTENTS

INTRODUCTION

The Old Biloxi Cemetery holds many secrets. The moss-draped oaks with twisted trunks and broken limbs stand watch over myriad tombs that date back to the 1800s. The cemetery is one of the oldest and most historic graveyards from Mobile to New Orleans. But like so many others, the old cemetery has fallen victim to the ravages of time and neglect. Its location, within walking distance of the gulf, has left the graves particularly vulnerable to the elements. Many of the tombs have suffered from the fierce storms that have battered the aging structures for over a century.

After Hurricane Katrina in 2005, one of the most powerful storms to hit the Gulf Coast, bones were strewn about the cemetery, with little respect for the dead. Headstones were broken, and concrete copings were shifted into unnatural shapes or completely destroyed. Some of the beautiful moss-draped oaks that had offered a shady respite from the blistering sun were ripped from their roots, toppling onto some of the very graves they had protected for generations. The fence that had served as a boundary between the peaceful land of the dead and the hectic world of the living was completely demolished, leaving pieces of brick and wrought iron strewn from the cemetery to the water's edge. The Old Biloxi Cemetery was ripped apart like it had never been before, and many questioned whether it could ever be put back together. The condition of the cemetery was particularly disturbing, as it is the resting place of some of the area's most prominent and historical figures.

Above: The Old Biloxi Cemetery was ripped apart by Hurricane Katrina. *Photograph by John Cuevas.*

Left: The Old Biloxi Cemetery is the resting place of some of the area's most prominent and historical figures. *Photograph by John Cuevas.*

The oldest upright, two-vault platform tomb in the Old Biloxi Cemetery is the resting place of Juan de Cuevas, known in coast history as the "Hero of Cat Island." Over the years, the old Cuevas tomb has suffered like many of the others. Some of the most devastating damage to the structure occurred during hurricane Camille in 1969, when the marble tablet that covered the entrance was cracked and broken in half. Areas of plaster that covered the sides of the tomb were chipped away. The mortar between the

Left: The oldest upright, two-vault platform tomb in the Old Biloxi Cemetery is the resting place of Juan de Cuevas, the hero of Cat Island. *Photograph by John Cuevas.*

Below: The old Cuevas tomb suffered devastating damage during hurricane Camille in 1969. *Photograph by John Cuevas.*

joints had crumbled, leaving many of the bricks loosely stacked, with some missing completely.

Recently, several concerned members of the Cuevas family recognized that something had to be done to save the old structure from its worsening condition. A group called the Descendants of Juan de Cuevas Family Association was formed for the purpose of saving one of the oldest and most historic tombs in the Old Biloxi Cemetery from further deterioration.

The members obtained a grant from the Mississippi Gulf Coast National Heritage Area, along with contributions from family members and friends, to finance the project. Nick Black of NOLA Cemetery Renewal, a prominent expert in tomb restoration from New Orleans, was employed to save the Cuevas tomb.

The old vault, which had been closed since the last burial over one hundred years ago, had to be reopened in order to complete the restoration. To protect and preserve the ancient remains inside the tomb, Dr. Marie Danforth, a professor of anthropology at the University of Southern Mississippi, along with her team of devoted researchers, were called in to carefully remove what was left of Juan de Cuevas and his wife, Marie. Riemann's, a local funeral home, offered to store the remains while the restoration work was being completed.

The project meant that the old tomb had to be virtually reconstructed. No tomb restoration of this magnitude and with this attention to detail has ever been undertaken on the Mississippi Gulf Coast, and definitely, no tomb restoration has ever been so meticulously documented. Professional photographers Jason Taylor and Chris Cahill were charged with taking a step-by-step photographic record of the restoration process. In addition, Cahill videotaped the complete project—from the beginning to the end—to produce a future documentary.

During the removal of the remains, a shocking secret was discovered. The tomb that, for over a century, was believed to only contain the remains of Juan de Cuevas and his wife was found to also contain the remains of a twenty-seven-year-old woman and a child that was estimated to be about five years old. Who was this mystery woman and infant? What was their connection to the Cuevas family? Why were they in the tomb? These are some of the intriguing secrets in the Old Biloxi Cemetery.

To understand the importance of the Juan de Cuevas tomb restoration, one must understand the significance of the Ladner/Cuevas family to the history of the greater Gulf Coast region. Juan de Cuevas is arguably one of the best-known settlers to have ever lived on the coast. His influence on the area goes far beyond his ownership of Cat Island and his legendary actions in the War of 1812; Juan de Cuevas is more importantly the patriarch of the largest founding family in South Mississippi.[1] There were only thirty families living between Mobile and New Orleans when Cuevas first came from Algámitas, Spain, in the late 1700s.[2] Now, it is a fact that an enormous number of coastal residents can trace their roots back to Juan de Cuevas and Cat Island. It has been rightfully said that Juan and his wife,

The marble tablet at the entrance to the Cuevas tomb. *Photograph by John Cuevas.*

Marie Ladner, can be considered the Adam and Eve of the Mississippi Gulf Coast. The eventual union between Juan's eleven children of Cat Island and the other newly transplanted Europeans resulted in the largest extended family in, possibly, the entire South. Through their children and their children's children, most of the original Europeans settlers became part of the Cuevas family, including notable personalities such as Pete Fountain, Hale Boggs, Cokie Roberts, Brett Favre, Diane Ladd, Laura Dern, Jimmy Buffett, William H. Macy and others who are all descendants of Juan de Cuevas.[3] The connection of so many to Cat Island and Juan de Cuevas is a cultural phenomenon.

Given the historical importance of the Old Biloxi Cemetery and the genealogical impact of the Cuevas family to the Mississippi Gulf Coast, this book is an important record. Not only was the Cuevas tomb restored and the identity of the young mystery woman and child uncovered, but the dramatic photographs by Jason and Chris accurately document the whole restoration process for future historians and gravers. The hope is that this book will inspire others to undertake similar projects to save these old tombs. The Old Biloxi Cemetery, like all of the other historic cemeteries in the country, have many deep and wonderful secrets to discover.

1
CEMETERIES IN AMERICA

Humans have both feared and worshipped death since the beginning of time. Rituals and religious practices have been developed in an attempt to explain and understand the mystery surrounding it. Most cultures today use cemeteries to memorialize the dead, not only out of respect for those who have passed on, but also as a therapeutic way for the living to deal with their grief and find closure. Monuments and memorials to the deceased give family and friends a place to visit and feel connected to the person they lost.

Cemeteries as we know them today are a relatively new idea. Our modern cemeteries, known as "garden cemeteries," developed out of necessity. As populations increased over time, European countries ran into problems with disposing of their dead. Originally, everyone wanted to be buried in their churchyards to be closer to God. Recognizing an opportunity to increase their coffers, churches began selling expensive plots inside the churches themselves, giving people the feeling of being even closer to the Almighty. It wasn't long, however, before churches and the churchyards were overflowing.[4]

Aside from those in the churchyard, some cemeteries are small family plots, isolated in the country, and still others are sanctioned areas at the edges of cities or towns. No matter the type, all cemeteries have one thing in common: they are filled with headstones, markers and mausoleums to help us remember our loved ones and tell future generations about the people who were buried there.

Wandering through the Old Biloxi Cemetery, one can feel the weight of history chiseled in the weathered stones. The old markers reveal secrets about the deceased and the times in which they lived. The practice of marking a grave goes back to the ancient Egyptians. In the Roman catacombs, early Christians were buried in slots along the walls of the subterranean tunnels. These niches were then sealed with a slab inscribed with the person's name, date of death and, usually, a religious symbol, such as a fish, which was the mark of early Christians. During the Victorian era (1837–1901), grave markers became very elaborate, fashioned after those of the ancient Greeks, Romans and Egyptians. After World War I, however, grave markers became simpler and less ornate. Plain wooden crosses or simple stone slabs carved with the deceased's name and an epitaph became the norm.

Other cultures practiced cremation, but the Christians didn't believe in cremation. They believed that the body should be kept intact, in readiness for the final resurrection. Burial in the church or the churchyard was the only way to dispose of the dead. In America, the churchyard remained the most common burial place through the end of the 1800s. Unfortunately, the stench and the spread of diseases made churchyard burials a problem. To address the crisis, cities began to buy large blocks of land outside the city limits where they could bury the bodies. The term *cemetery* is Greek for "sleeping place," and indeed, cemeteries can be thought of as sleeping places for those who have passed away.

While city cemeteries are the norm today, private family cemeteries were originally more common. In early America, people would stake out a plot of land somewhere on their property to begin a family burial site—usually in a wooded area on the edge of their farm. It was not uncommon to allow other families to bury their loved ones in the same plot. Some of these plots became real cemeteries as more families were buried on their neighbors' properties. The Krohn Cemetery at 16299 Krohn Road in Vancleave, the Moran Cemetery at 10059 Santa Cruz Avenue in D'Iberville and the Quave Cemetery at 3315 West Race Track Road also in D'Iberville are just three examples of these small family cemeteries that have survived. There are many more family burial sites like these along the Gulf Coast. In many cases, the early markers were wooden crosses. In a very short time, these crosses rotted away, often leaving the graves unmarked and forgotten.

The movement toward garden-like cemeteries spread to America after the creation of the Père Lachaise Cemetery in Paris, France. The cemetery opened in 1804; it was the first garden-style cemetery and is the largest municipal cemetery in Paris.[5] The neoclassical architect Alexandre-

Theodore Brongniart (February 1739–June 6, 1813) designed the cemetery. He used English gardens as his inspiration, with uneven paths and diverse trees and plants. He lined the way with carved graves. His plan was to include various funerary monuments, but in the beginning, only one was ever built. It was the tomb of Count Jean-Henry-Louis Greffulhe (May 21, 1774–February 23, 1820), a French banker and politician. Père Lachaise has become the most visited cemetery in the world, with over 3.5 million visitors a year.[6] After Père Lachaise, people began to appreciate the peaceful setting that the garden-style atmosphere provided for families who wanted to remember their loved ones.

The first garden-style cemetery in America was the Mount Auburn Cemetery, created in 1831 in Cambridge, Massachusetts. Designed by Dr. Jacob Bigelow (February 27, 1787–January 10, 1879) and Henry A.S. Dearborn (March 3, 1783–July 29, 1851), it featured an Egyptian-style gate and fence, a Norman tower and a granite chapel.[7] It was an immediate success, inspiring similar cemeteries in cities throughout the United States. These garden-style cemeteries were the exact opposite of crowded churchyards, where a person's status in society dictated the location of their grave.

New "garden cemeteries" became popular not only as burial grounds but also as public recreation areas. They developed into beautiful, peaceful areas where the dead could rest far away from the hustle and bustle of the cities. These places were beautifully landscaped areas where people could relax and stroll around the grounds and even picnic. These cemeteries became the forerunners of our modern parks.[8]

The Victorians can be credited with making cemeteries what they are today. They created a park-like atmosphere where family outings and picnics were held. The people of that era were more comfortable with the subject of death than we are today, since dying was a part of most of their lives. Because of such devastating diseases as yellow fever and cholera, few people lived past forty. So, to be close to their deceased relatives, families would gather in the cemeteries to talk and visit with the living and the dead. A man in 1884 commented on why his family chose to eat in the cemetery: "We are going to keep Thanksgivin' with our father as [though he] was as live and hearty this day [as] last year."[9]

As cemeteries became popular hangouts, it became important to show plots off to friends. This effort to "keep up with the Joneses" resulted in the creation of overstated mausoleums and ornate tombstones. This trend toward architectural gingerbread and flashy structural elements reflected the gaudiness of the Victorian era. This was the most extravagant architectural period in the United States, in which some of the most lavish and beautiful vaults were created.

Like all fads, dining in cemeteries began to diminish by the early twentieth century. Advancements in medicine reduced the number of early deaths, while the proliferation of parks throughout the country offered a more inviting place for relaxation and picnics. Today, there are only a few cemeteries with enough available land for large gatherings, and most current city policies will no longer allow for picnics.

Over the past several years, visiting cemeteries has become a hobby for a large number of people. This activity is so widespread that the people who participate have their own name. They have become known as "gravers."[10] The idea of visiting cemeteries as a form of entertainment may, at first, seem somewhat twisted, but for those who are seeking information, it is more than something ghoulish. It is an informal classroom that not only entertains but educates. The gravers' interests can include a wide variety of topics. Some are genealogists who visit various cemeteries to take notes and fill in the missing branches of family trees. Others plan their trips around the burial places of public figures or entertainers. Patriotic gravers might visit the resting places of the soldiers who died in the Civil War, World War II or some other military conflict. Gravers who are preservationist actually visit cemeteries with bleach in hand to scrub and clean the aging stones. In general, gravers consider it fun to visit cemeteries. Some have no other agenda than to just stroll among the tombstones or just hang out.

Hardcore gravers have created a culture around their interests in documenting the dead. They collect cemetery jokes and stories from the tombstones, in addition to offering advice on a graver's needed supplies, such as the proper kneepads, high-resolution digital camera, tracing paper for rubbings and shaving cream to wipe across worn inscriptions to make the words more legible. The more serious gravers create individual records for each of the deceased by transcribing the information directly from the headstone. They dismiss the use of obituaries to gather information, emphasizing, instead, the importance of seeing the actual tombstones. This means that a trip to the cemetery cannot be avoided. Those researchers who carelessly collect information in the comfort of their living rooms from newspapers instead of tombstones are called "ploppers." They believe that ploppers most often enter erroneous information about names, dates or burial locations. Serious gravers accuse them of being more interested in the number of records they collect rather than the quality of their work.

Over the years, certain customs have developed around cemeteries and burial sites in Louisiana and in the old communities along the Gulf Coast. One of the most popular traditions has been the celebration of All Saints' Day and All Souls' Day. These are the results of the strong Roman Catholic influences throughout the area. All Saints' Day honors the saints. There are evening masses celebrated in cemeteries and a blessing of the graves by the attending priest. All Souls' Day celebrates families and friends who have passed away. It is a festive time when communities come together to visit with friends, clean and decorate the graves with flowers and pay respect to the deceased.[11]

The above-ground tombs are a tradition brought to the area by the Spanish. As Lucy L. McCann of the Louisiana State Board stated, "Placing burial vaults above ground or partially above ground is an aesthetic or cultural preference that has nothing to do with the law or the water table." The first cemetery in New Orleans was St. Peter, which was an in-ground cemetery near the French Quarter. When it was filled, St. Louis I was created. It was an above-ground burial site designed after the old cemeteries in Spain. The use of vaults was a practical matter, as they allowed for more than one burial in the same spot.

Another popular custom was to bury the deceased with their head facing west and feet facing east. According to Christian and Jewish tradition, the Messiah will return to this world from the east, and the person would want their body to rise from the grave facing the Messiah.

One custom was the "year and a day" rule." It was tradition not to open a tomb until at least one year and a day had passed since the last burial. This was a practical step that allowed enough time for the previous body to completely decompose before another one was placed in the same tomb. The extreme heat and humidity that builds up in these tombs accelerates the decomposition process. This custom has been followed for generations. But recently, the rule has been changed to two years and a day as an extra precautionary measure.

These customs were also practiced in the Old Biloxi Cemetery. Several of the tombs have been used for multiple burials, and all of the deceased in the original section were buried with their feet toward the east.

To some, cemeteries are mysterious places, full of superstitions and sorrow. But cemeteries should not be thought of as spooky places or even as places of sadness and loss; rather, they should actually be appreciated as windows to the past.

2

THE OLD BILOXI CEMETERY

The Old Biloxi Cemetery is located at 1166 Irish Hill Drive on a high bluff overlooking the gulf, only a stone's throw away from the hectic traffic of Highway 90. The serenity of this historic site is a welcome contrast to the glitz and glitter of the twenty-four-hour casinos just minutes away. A visit to the cemetery is a pleasant way to spend an hour or an entire day, listening the gulf breeze rustling through the trees while getting to know some of the men and women who laid the foundation for today's Mississippi Gulf Coast.

The Old Biloxi Cemetery officially opened on November 27, 1844, when the family of Louis Lalanzette Fayard donated approximately six acres of his land to the city for use as a graveyard.[12] The cemetery was part of a much larger parcel that had been granted to Fayard by the U.S. government on April 25, 1812, and was already being used for burials when it was deeded to the city.[13]

No records have been found to say when the first burials took place on the site, but some historians believe the area was probably used for burial as far back as the early 1700s, when Biloxi was the planned capital of the Louisiana Territory. The site of the Old Biloxi Cemetery is on land near the proposed Fort Louis, where small, scattered groups of people had been living since the French first arrived. Some most likely would have been buried near their homes, while others might have chosen the land near the old Biloxi Cemetery because of the site's protective elevation. This offered some security from storm surges, and its proximity to the newly intended

Fort Louis made it an ideal spot for the early French settlers to dispose of their dead.[14]

From the very beginning, the French had to endure horrible living conditions. Hundreds and probably thousands died between 1719 and 1721 from disease, a lack of food and the raw conditions of the undeveloped territory. Many died as a disastrous result of John Law (1671–1729) and his Mississippi Company, while others died from the yellow fever epidemic of 1853. John Law imported hundreds of people from Germany and other European countries who had been deceived into believing they were headed for paradise.

The French had arrived on the coast on April 9, 1682. When French explorer René-Robert Cavelier de la Salle (1643–1687) became the first to reach the mouth of the Mississippi River, he claimed the entire basin for France, quickly planting a cross as a physical marker of French possession, naming the new territory La Louisiane in honor of King Louis XIV (1638–1715).[15]

La Salle believed that the only way to retain control of this vast region would be to colonize the area. After convincing the king this was the right thing to do, he started the first settlement at the mouth of the Mississippi River. Louis XIV commissioned Pierre Le Moyne Sieur d'Iberville (1661–1706), a thirty-seven-year-old from Quebec, to return to the mouth of the Mississippi River and set up a new settlement.

D'Iberville, along with his nineteen-year-old brother, Jean Baptiste Le Moyne de Bienville (1680–1767), a group of about two hundred colonists, two armed ships and two smaller vessels, departed from LaRochelle, France. On their initial arrival in the gulf, the French explorers searched the shallow waters along the coast for a harbor that was deep enough to accommodate their large ships. On February 10, 1699, they discovered the Ship Island Harbor.[16]

After a camp was set up on Ship Island, the crew determined that the mouth of the Mississippi River was not an ideal place to build a fort. They finally decided that Biloxi was the best site and returned on March 30, 1699, to begin construction. The fort was named after the French minister of the navy Jean-Fréderic Phélypeaux, comte de Maurepas (1701–1781).[17]

The first summer at Fort Maurepas in Biloxi (known today as Ocean Springs) was almost unbearable, as the young colony was forced to endure the extreme heat and draught of 1700. The people suffered, as the food crops dried up from the sizzling heat and lack of rain. The insects were particularly bad that year, and the men were attacked by swarms of mosquitoes, horse flies and other biting insects. Boredom, complicated by dysentery and fever, caused the men's morale to tank. The threat of alligators and snakes was a constant concern, while the shrinking of the food supply was hastened by an increasing number of Canadians continuing to arrive on the coast.

Meanwhile, the British were becoming a greater threat because of the War of Spanish Succession (1701–1713). D'Iberville, who had been in France to report on the colony's progress, returned on December 5, 1701, with orders to move the Biloxi colony to a site on the Mobile River that was closer to their Spanish allies for support. All weapons and supplies were ordered to be moved immediately to warehouses on Dauphin Island. The French feared hostilities from the British.[18]

In August 1717, a severe hurricane devastated the Mobile area, putting an end to the capital in Mobile. This forced Bienville to seek yet another capital for the Louisiana Territory. He founded the new settlement he called New Orleans in a bend of the Mississippi River. Bienville's choice was not well received by the superior council of the colony. Believing that the port at Ship Island was more important, the French vetoed New Orleans, and the capital was moved from Mobile back to Biloxi, near the original site of Fort Maurepas. A year later, the colony moved again, this time, across the bay to the bluff overlooking the gulf near the Old Biloxi Cemetery location. The new settlement was called "New Biloxi." This eventually became the present-day city of Biloxi. The council gave orders to begin the construction of Fort Louis facing the Mississippi Sound.

It just so happened that during all of this indecision about the capital, the French economy was beginning to collapse. France's financial disaster made it impossible for the king to continue supporting the Louisiana colony. As an absolute monarch, Louis XIV was an extravagant spender. He spent half of the French treasury maintaining his palace at Versailles after spending $100 million on its construction. His lavish lifestyle was out of control, with no laws to keep it in check. The king imposed taxes on the country to increase revenue, but these taxes placed an unfair burden on the peasants and the middle class, since the nobility and clergy were exempt from paying any taxes. This unjust taxation would eventually result in rebellion and the French Revolution (1789–1799).

Looking for a way to reverse the downward spiral, Louis XIV awarded a grant to Antoine Crozat, Marquis du Châtel (1650–1738), the wealthiest man in France, to save the colony and thus save France from a financial catastrophe. Crozat was given absolute control and full responsibility of the Louisiana Territory. Promising to make the new settlement profitable,

Crozat saw the venture as a way to increase his personal wealth. Crozat's efforts failed. His botched attempt only made the financial problems of the country worse, leaving France deeper in debt.

The colony continued to cause a strain on the country's finances. In desperation, the government was willing to try anything. A Scottish financier, John Law (1671–1729) presented his plan that promised he could successfully turn the economy around where Crozat had failed.[19] King Louis XIV was not quick to act, but on his death, the Duc d'Orleans, under the new king, Louis XV, awarded Law power over the Louisiana Territory.

John Law and his associates took over the colony in 1717, calling their group John Law's Company of the West, which became popularly known as the Mississippi Company. A grant was given to Law, giving him complete control.

The Mississippi Company was set up as a form of corporation so the group could sell stock. John Law was elected CEO, and a board of directors was appointed. In order to get investors, a slick promotional campaign was developed, with deceptive brochures and unsupported stock. This set off a frenzy of speculation for the cash-strapped country. The persuasive materials presented the Gulf Coast as a Garden of Eden.[20] But even with all of the hype, Law was still having trouble getting people to sign up.

Law accomplished this monumental goal by taking unwilling participants by force. Disorderly soldiers, black sheep of distinguished families, paupers, prostitutes and even unsuspecting peasants who happened to stray into Paris were swept up and transported by force to the Louisiana Territory. There were some who chose to settle on the Gulf Coast, and to those individuals, Law offered free land, provisions and transportation to the new territory.[21] This mass of new immigrants landed on Dauphin Island, and they were totally shocked by the horrendous conditions they discovered. They were crowded, unsheltered and unfed; some grew sick, and many died.[22] Researchers believe that the Old Biloxi Cemetery was the site of many of their burials.

Those who were respectable participants and who had chosen to come voluntarily were disheartened to find themselves thrown together with the hardened criminals and misfits who had been forced to make the trip.[23] To relieve the situation, groups of volunteers were distributed throughout the coast to Pascagoula, Biloxi, Ship Island and other locations. There was hardly enough food to even feed the few soldiers who were left to defend the new colony.

The squalid conditions were so unbearable that the good people and the bad were anxious to leave Biloxi as soon as possible.[24] New Orleans benefited

REYNOIR
AMELIE REYNOIR 1840 — 1874
LOUIS CONEY DUMONTAT 1790 — 1874
ANTOINE REYNOIR 1846 — 1879
LOUISE ELISABETH REYNOIR 1801 — 1891
ARTHUR REYNOIR 1832 — 1897
NELLIE BOYLE REYNOIR 1874 — 1915
ROSA DORSEY REYNOIR 1842 — 1917
LOUISE REYNOIR CAMORS 1873 — 1923
FREDERICK A REYNOIR 1869 — 1925
JOHN B. REYNOIR 1876 — 1931
CLOTILDE REVOL REYNOIR 1893 — 1965

Opposite: Frederick "Arthur" Reynoir. *Photograph by Chris Cahill.*

Above: The marble door of the impressive eight-foot-tall Reynoir family vault. *Photograph by Chris Cahill.*

and prospered from this onslaught of disgruntled immigrants and wealthy elite to become, at one time, the third-largest city in the United States.[25]

Disease was another major cause of death on the Gulf Coast. The yellow fever epidemic of 1796 was a sixty-seven-year struggle that took the lives of approximately one out of every twelve persons in New Orleans alone.[26] There are no burial records before 1841, so without any surviving headstones, the identities of the dead are secrets that are lost forever. Historians believe that many of these burials took place in the vicinity of the Old Biloxi Cemetery, but where these graves are located is one of the more enduring secrets.

The Reynoir tomb contains the bodies of over twenty family members. *Photograph by Chris Cahill.*

Spanish governor Estéban Miró (1744–1795) persuaded New Orleans officials to implement the wall vault system that was popular in Spain at the time. The practice of burial in vaults quickly became popular, particularly among the wealthier families who could afford larger and more ornate tombs. For all but the indigent, above-ground tombs became the rule, including in the Old Biloxi Cemetery.

At first, the tombs were not fancy or decorative. Mostly, they were simple but functional. Years later, architects were hired to provide elaborate tombs for the wealthy and elite. One of the first in the Old Biloxi Cemetery that incorporated the Spanish method was that of Juan de Cuevas (1762–1849.)

The Spanish system of burial that was adopted by Governor Miró allowed for multiple burials in the same vault. One of the most dramatic examples of multiple burials in a single vault in the Old Biloxi Cemetery was the impressive eight-foot-high Reynoir family vault that contains a list of names and burial dates engraved on both sides of the tablet. There were so many names on the marble door that it had to be flipped around, and eleven new names were added to the other side. The tomb had been built of Georgia marble in 1896 for Frederick "Arthur" Reynoir (1832–1897), a successful land speculator in Biloxi, and contained the bodies of over twenty family members. The last member of the Reynoir family to be interred there was placed there in 2013.

3

NOTEWORTHY BURIALS IN THE OLD BILOXI CEMETERY

Among those buried in the Old Biloxi Cemetery are heroes and villains, rich men and poor, but mostly, they were just ordinary people whose names reflect the heritage of most of the area's residents. All deserve recognition, but there are far too many to acknowledge them all. The following are only some of the notable people who are buried in the Old Biloxi Cemetery, with a brief summary of their lives.

Edward Charles Edmond "Edouard" Barq Sr.: Creator of Barq's Root Beer

What would fried catfish, a shrimp po'boy or a big bowl of seafood gumbo be without a cold bottle of Barq's? Edward Charles Barq, the creator of Barq's root beer, the unofficial soft drink of the Mississippi Gulf Coast, was born in New Orleans on March 4, 1871.[27]

Edouard, as he was known, was the youngest of six children, born to Jules Auguste Barq of France and Marie Georgine Savonnière of New Orleans. His brothers and sisters were Felix Charles "Gaston," Anaisi Amelie, Charles Paul Auguste, Delphine Marie Eugenie and Jules Auguste Barq Jr. Edouard was only two years old when his father died. After his father's death, his mother returned to her family in France, where the children attended school. Young Edouard pursued a study of flavor chemistry in college, learning from some of the greatest authorities in Paris.

Edward Barq. *Photograph by Chris Cahill.*

With the growing prospects of France's involvement in World War I, Edouard and his younger brother Gaston fled the country to avoid military service. They returned to New Orleans, where they opened their first business. They began bottling carbonated water under the name Barq's Brothers Bottling Company. As a sideline, they began developing their own soft drinks. Experimenting with several flavors, their most successful was an orange soda called Orangine. Entering the drink in a competition at the 1893 Chicago World's Fair, the Barq brothers won a gold medal. Encouraged by the success of Orangine, they decided to continue their work in developing soft drinks. Unfortunately, Edouard's brother and business partner died shortly after Orangine hit the market, and he was never able to share in the drink's success.

In 1897, after Gaston's death, Edouard Barq closed the company in New Orleans and moved to Biloxi, where he opened a new business called the Biloxi Artesian Bottling Works. While in New Orleans, he had met a local girl, Elodie Graugnard. Once settled in Biloxi, the couple married on May 15, 1898.[28]

During the winter months, he worked as a chemist on Louisiana sugar plantations for extra income, but in the summer, he would return to Biloxi, to his business of bottling artesian water. He also bottled several fruit drinks and soda, while continuing to develop his own flavors of soft drinks. It was during this time that he first created his famous root beer.[29]

Most historians cite 1898 as the year that Barq's root beer was created, mainly because that is the year the company was founded in Biloxi.[30] In fact, Edouard did not begin making his root beer until 1900, shortly after a Mr. Court began working with the company. Since Barq spoke very little English and kept all of his notes in French, it has been difficult to determine the exact date the drink debuted. With Mr. Court's help, Barq's root beer became very successful all along the coast. The drink had become so popular that Edouard opened a second location in Gulfport.

The drink known as root beer was originally created in 1876 by Mr. Charles Elmer Hires. Hires originally planned on calling his soda drink root tea but changed the name to root beer in a marketing ploy to appeal to the local workers in the Pennsylvania coal mines.[31] Edouard Barq came into conflict with the Hires company over the use of the name "root beer." To avoid any possible lawsuits with the Hires Root Beer Company, Edouard simply called his drink Barq's. The company's famous slogan became, "Drink Barq's, it's good." Eventually, the dispute was resolved, and Edouard's soda was allowed to be called Barq's root beer.[32]

Barq's formula was different from Hires's. While Hires and other root beers incorporated sassafras, Barq's used sarsaparilla as its base. Sarsaparilla plants were used in several popular drinks in the late 1800s.[33] Barq's also used less sugar and caffeine than any other brands at that time. Barq's most unique identifying difference is its "bite." This is due to the higher amount of carbonation that is found in Barq's root beer than in any other similar soft drink.[34]

In 1907, a Mr. Hartner joined Edouard as a partner in the company. Hartner proved to be a disaster and was forced to leave the company in 1910. Edouard regained control but not before having to close his Gulfport operation.

When Mr. Edouard Barq Sr. died on May 23, 1943, his two sons, Edward Charles Edmond Barq Jr. and Edward Adolphe Barq, took control of the company. The two brothers ran the company until the death of Edward Jr. in 1970, when his two children, Ella and William, inherited the company. In 1976, the company was sold to two businessmen, John Oudt and John Koerner. In 1995, they sold Barq's root beer to the Coca-Cola Company. The Coca-Cola Company made Barq's root beer the number-one root beer soda in the country.[35]

Edouard's wife, Elodie Graugnard, died in 1968. She and Mr. Edouard Barq were both buried in the Old Biloxi Cemetery.

CHARLES ALBERT BESSEY: HERO OF CUSTER'S LAST STAND IN THE GREAT SIOUX WARS

Corporal Charles Albert Bessey was a hero in the Great Sioux Wars of 1876–77. Born on November 6, 1848, in Reading, Pennsylvania, he married Mary Elizabeth McCabe (1868–1935) in 1892. Bessey served in Company A of the Third Calvary Regiment of the United States Army. Nicknamed "Brave Rifles," the regiment was constituted in the regular army in May 1846 as the Regiment of Mounted Riflemen.[36] He received the military's highest award, the Medal of Honor, for his heroic actions in the Indian Wars.

War broke out in 1876 between the U.S. government, the Northern Cheyenne and the Lakota Sioux Natives led by Sitting Bull. The United States was trying to take over the Black Hills, a small range of isolated mountains that extended from the plains in South Dakota into Wyoming.[37] Gold had been discovered there, and settlers were beginning to encroach on the land that belonged to the Natives in search of the gold. The Sioux and Cheyenne refused to allow the government to take over their land.

One day during the war, Bessey and two army privates were repairing a telegraph line running from Fort Laramie to Fetterman in the eastern Wyoming Territory, when they received word that three cattle herders were attacked by Cheyenne Natives near Elkhorn Creek. Although Bessey and his two men were wounded in the skirmish, these three men faced fourteen Cheyenne warriors and were able to force the release of the herders. One of

Charles Bessey. *Photograph by Chris Cahill.*

the most famous of the many battles of the Great Sioux War was the Battle of the Little Bighorn. It became popularly known as Custer's Last Stand.[38]

The war that had begun under Ulysses S. Grant (April 27, 1822–July 23, 1885) continued under President Rutherford B. Hayes (October 4, 1822–January 17, 1893). An agreement was finally signed in 1877 that resulted in the permanent establishment of Native reservations.[39]

On May 15, 1890, thirteen years later, Corporal Charles Albert Bessey received Medal of Honor for his heroic actions. Bessey's official Medal reads:

> *While scouting with 4 men and attacked in ambush by 14 hostile Indians, held his ground, 2 of his men being wounded, and kept up the fight until himself wounded in the side, and then went to the assistance of his wounded comrades.*[40]

Charles Bessey retired from the army in 1899 but not before being promoted to sergeant. He also became the chief musician of his regiment.

He died on June 4, 1909, at the age of sixty from kidney failure, believed caused by the wound he suffered during his battle with the Natives at Elkhorn Creek. Later, his family donated his medal to the Third Cavalry Museum in Fort Hood, Texas.

RAYMOND CAILLAVET: MAYOR OF BILOXI AND CIVIC LEADER, CREDITED WITH EXTENDING THE BEACHFRONT ROAD

Raymond Caillavet was born in 1838 in Biloxi. His grandfather Symphorian Caillavet (1746–1806) first arrived in the United States from his home in Bordeaux, France, around 1788 and settled in Opelousas, Louisiana, where he married Rose Marie Carriere (1766–circa 1855), a native of New Orleans. The couple made their home in Opelousas, where their two sons, Louis-Francois Arbau Caillavet (1793–1860) and Adolph Caillavet (circa 1803–1842), were born.

Raymond's father, Louis-Francois Arbau Caillavet, moved from Opelousas to Biloxi, marking the first arrival of the Caillavet family on the Mississippi Gulf Coast around 1812. In Biloxi, he married Marguerite Fayard, the daughter of Jean Baptist Fayard Jr. (1752–1816) and Angelique Ladner (1753–1830), members of two of the oldest families on the Mississippi Gulf Coast.[41]

Raymond's father was fluent in both English and French. Very few people on the coast could read or write at that time. Because of this, Raymond was asked to read and explain various legal contracts, acting as a notary in legal matters and land contracts. This led to his election as treasurer of the Harrison County Board of Police, what is the board of supervisors today.[42] This community service would have a profound impact on Raymond's future career.

Raymond's parents had five children. Their oldest daughter, Rose Desiree Caillavet (September 20, 1813), would later marry Charles Ferdinand Cuevas (1811–October 27, 1894), the son of Juan de Cuevas known in coast history as the "Hero of Cat Island."

Raymond Caillavet, known as "Medeaux," worked as a carpenter like his father, Francois Arbau, until joining the Confederate army. He enlisted as a private in Company E (Biloxi Rifles), Third Mississippi Infantry, CSA. Company E had been put together mainly for the defense of the Mississippi Sound.[43]

Raymond Caillavet. *Photograph by Chris Cahill.*

During his service, Raymond was stationed in New Orleans. While he was there, he met Zelina Jonchere. Zelina was born in New Orleans on November 24, 1841, although her parents were from France.[44] Raymond "Medeaux" Caillavet married Zelina while he was still stationed in New Orleans. Their first two children, Marie Blanche Caillavet (1865–1940), John Caillavet (circa 1867–circa 1870) were born in New Orleans before the family returned to live in Biloxi in 1869. On settling in Biloxi, they became members of the Catholic Church of the Nativity of the Blessed Virgin Mary.[45]

On February 26, 1869, Raymond bought a piece of property fronting North Street in Biloxi from his father for $200. It was eighty-five feet wide and two hundred feet deep. It was bounded to the north by North Street, east by Mrs. Lefaure's land, south by Mr. Cook's land and west by Cuevas Street, next door to other members of his family. His parents lived on the street, as did his younger brother John. Charles Cuevas and his wife, Rose Desiree Caillavet, lived next door to the Caillavets on the street that was named for Charles's father, Juan de Cuevas of Cat Island.[46]

The land on which the Caillavets's home was located was deeded to the city for a road by Louis-Francois Arbau Caillavet, Raymond's father. The street was originally thirty-seven feet wide and ran from the beachfront all the way to Back Bay, but after years of alternate paths, the street had become almost unidentifiable. Trying to redefine the street was almost impossible because the records were destroyed by a fire. In 1896, Biloxi alderman Nash was able to determine the original location. The old road was given the name of Caillavet Street in honor of the Caillavet family who were the original owners of the land on which it was built. It is on this street that Raymond and Zelina raised their seven children: Marie Blanche Caillavet (1865–1940), John Caillavet (circa 1867–circa 1870), Aristide Bertrand Caillavet (1868–1898), Emma Rose C. Murray (circa 1869–1955), Alice C. Bellande (1872–1955), Edward Caillavet (1874–1923), Clarissa Rita Caillavet (1877–1885), William Caillavet (1879–1940), Lillian C. Holley (1883–1967) and Louise C. Morgan (1881–1965).

After the Civil War ended, Raymond came back to the coast, mostly working as a butcher until he became involved in local politics. With his grandfather Louis as an inspiration, he ran for the position of justice of the peace in District 1, the same position his father had held. Raymond held the office from 1873 to 1875. After his term expired, he went on to become the coroner and ranger from 1875 to 1877. Encouraged by his family and friends, he ran for mayor and won. Raymond served as Biloxi's mayor for two terms from 1877 to 1882, having won a second term in January 1879 by defeating his opponent, J.R. Harkness.[47]

Not able to run for a third term, he served as street commissioner of Biloxi, during which time he is credited with extending the beach road from Porter Avenue to a point near the Biloxi City Cemetery. This section was connected with the beach road that had already been finished from Mississippi City. In October 1883, the *Pascagoula Democrat-Star* praised Raymond Caillavet for his great foresight, stating: "Mr. Caillavet removed trees and stumps, but when completed, the road had the appearance of a 'long avenue shaded on both sides.' The city fathers could not have appointed a more efficient man for commissioner than the present incumbent."[48]

After his success as street commissioner, Caillavet ran again for coroner and ranger, this time, serving from 1889 to 1891. In 1894, he was elected as a city councilman, serving until 1895. By 1888, his brother John also became active in politics, serving as a supervisor for District 1 of Harrison County.

Raymond Caillavet died on February 16, 1898. His wife, Zelina, died five years later, on March 15, 1903. They were both buried in the Old Biloxi Cemetery.

JAMES PARKS CALDWELL: COFOUNDER OF SIGMA CHI FRATERNITY

James Parks Caldwell, a cofounder of Sigma Chi fraternity, was born to Dr. William W. Caldwell and Isabella H. Parks on March 27, 1841, in Monroe, Ohio. There are two interesting points about James Caldwell that should be noted: James was only fourteen years old when he and three of his fellow students at Miami University in Oxford, Ohio, created the new Sigma Chi fraternity, and he was also the only one of the other founders of Sigma Chi who joined the Confederacy in the War Between the States.

According to his friends, James Caldwell was a brilliant and sensitive person. Benjamin Piatt Runkle, a close friend and one of the fraternity's founders, gave his impression of James Parks Caldwell:

> *Jimmie Caldwell was born with a wonderful brain and a strangely sensitive and delicate organization. He was, from his childhood, one of the most lovable of God's creations. Strong men who have become hardened to tender feeling and sympathetic sentiment remember and love him. Somehow, he seemed closely akin to all of us. I roomed and cared for him for more than a year. Our holidays were spent in the fields and along the streams, one of us carrying a gun or fishing rod, but Caldwell his copy of Poe or Shakespeare. His contributions, essays, poems, plays and stories read in the literary hall, in the chapter meetings and on Saturdays before the whole corps of students, were the most remarkable productions that I ever heard. Few of us escaped the pointed witticisms that flowed from his pen or ever lost the nicknames that he gave us in his dramas. He never seemed to study as other boys. What he knew appeared to be his intuitively. He wrote Latin and Greek poetry, and he was more widely versed in literature and more accurate in his knowledge than any other student in the college. He left the university with the respect and the wholehearted affection of every soul from president to janitor.*

Caldwell was a brilliant student who easily breezed through all of the academic courses that were offered at his school, including Latin and advanced math. Because of this outstanding accomplishment, he was allowed to enter Miami University at the age of thirteen. He graduated from the university within three years.[49]

Literary societies were an important part of college social life before the Civil War. These distinctive social groups were the beginning of college

James Parks Caldwell. *Photograph by Chris Cahill.*

fraternities and sororities, although they were more academic than the fraternities and sororities of today. They would often present original poetry, music and essays as part of the groups' events. Much of their activities consisted of formal debates on popular issues of the day, including slavery. Many of the members saw these groups as stepping-stones into politics.[50] Whitelaw Reid (October 27, 1837–December 15, 1912), one of the members, for example, became the vice presidential nominee in the 1892 U.S. election as well as the voice of the Republican Party. He was later appointed ambassador to France and Great Britain.[51]

In 1854, a disagreement developed between the twelve members of the Kappa chapter of the Delta Kappa Epsilon fraternity at Miami over the nomination for poet in the Erodelphian Literary Society. Not all members of the chapter supported this choice. Six of the members, led by Whitelaw Reid, supported the candidate, while four of the other six felt he was not qualified. James Parks Caldwell, one of the four, along with Issac M. Jordan, Benjamin Piatt Runkle and Franklin Howard Scobey, actually supported another man who was not even a member of the fraternity. Two other students, Thomas Cowan Bell and Daniel William Cooper, joined the four in the opposition, although they were not even members of the Erodelphian Literary Society. This split the fraternity evenly, with six members on each side. The arguments became so heated that it cost the group their friendships.[52]

In 1855, a meeting was held between Bell, Caldwell, Cooper, Jordan, Runkle and Scobey to try to resolve the conflict. Also attending were Whitelaw Reid and Minor Millikin from a different fraternity in nearby Hamilton, Ohio. Millikin took over the meeting and presented a plan that he and Reid had devised. They proposed that Runkle and Scobey be expelled from the group, since they were the leaders of the opposition. Needless to say, Runkle and the others stormed out of the room.

In April 1855, the parent chapter of Delta Kappa Epsilon at Yale stepped into the conflict and expelled Bell, Caldwell, Cooper, Jordan, Runkle and Scobey. The men immediately began making plans to form a new fraternity.[53]

William Lewis Lockwood became a new member of the group. He had just started at the university and had not yet joined a fraternity. His remarkable organizational skills proved to be a great asset to the success of the new project. He was responsible for setting up the structure of the new fraternity, much of which still exists today. On Commencement Day at Miami University, June 28, 1844, the seven founding members of Sigma Chi announced their new fraternity.[54]

After graduation, James Parks Caldwell went to work in the law offices of Judge James Clark in Hamilton, Ohio. Judge Clark had family connections in Panola County, Mississippi. James wanted to move south, so he took advantage of Judge Clark's help and moved to Mississippi. He soon became the principal of Palmetto Academy in Panola.

Although he was a northerner, he felt a loyalty to his newly adopted state. At twenty years old, he enlisted in the Confederate artillery, fighting in Mississippi and Louisiana. In 1863, he was captured and remained a prisoner for the rest of the war.[55]

At the end of the war, he returned to Palmetto Academy, serving again as its principal. He was later admitted to the bar in Mississippi and practiced law in various places, like California and Wyoming, before returning to Mississippi for good in 1888. He settled on the coast in Mississippi City, Gulfport and Biloxi, where he became a well-known authority on land law and titles going back to the era when the French and Spanish controlled the coast.[56]

James Parks Caldwell died on April 5, 1912, and was buried in the Old Biloxi Cemetery.

Juan José de Cuevas: The "Hero of Cat Island" in the Battle of New Orleans

Juan José de Cuevas was born in Algámitas, Spain, on July 8, 1762, in the diocese of Málaga. The village is in the autonomous region of Andalucía in the province of Sevilla, near the Costa del Sol.[57] He was the son of Don Pedro de Cuevas and Ysabel Bautista.[58]

Although much has been written about Juan de Cuevas, very little is known about him personally, and even less is known about his wife, Marie. Juan was about five feet, ten inches tall, somewhat taller than the average man of that time.[59] Like most of his other countrymen, he had coal black hair and a ruddy complexion that was the combination of his Mediterranean skin and the unrelenting southern sun of the Gulf Coast. He was fit and trim with firm muscles, a testimony to his hard work, and yet, his personality was as gentle as the summer breeze that drifted off the Mississippi Sound. His bearing was that of a nobleman, and he carried himself with grace and dignity. Although he was slow to anger, this gentle man was someone to reckon with. Everyone who knew Juan de Cuevas loved and respected him.[60]

Although Juan had little formal education, he was a very astute businessman. By all accounts, his herd of black cattle had made him a rich man, but it was not his livestock that ultimately made him wealthy. It was the sale of Cat Island that was the turning point in his life. He had the foresight to see that the future was on the mainland and not on the barrier islands. He had no intention of ever leaving his home, but he recognized that his children had moved on and would never return to live on the island again. He, therefore, accepted the deal proposed by Judah Benjamin, the secretary of state of the Confederate States of America, to purchase Cat Island. Cuevas sold the island with a life estate, which allowed him and Marie to live there in their island home for the rest of their lives as if it were still their own. The sale of Cat Island in 1837 made him one of the wealthiest men on the Gulf Coast at that time.

Judah Benjamin, the secretary of state of the Confederate States of America, purchased Cat Island from Juan de Cuevas. *Public domain.*

Juan was from a titled family in Spain. His father, Don Pedro, held the title of

Algámitas, Spain, the home of Juan de Cuevas. *Photograph by John Cuevas.*

Hidalgo de Carta. This was the lowest title of nobility granted by the king. The rank of hidalgo had no political significance but allowed its members certain privileges, such as the use of the title "Don" and considerable exemption from taxation. Along with the title, Don Pedro was given a large amount of tax-free land in Algámitas, on which the Cuevas family made their living by growing olives. Today, the same Cuevas land continues to produce some of the best olives in the valley, making the family one of the wealthiest in the village.

By the early nineteenth century, the title of hidalgo had entirely disappeared, along with the social status that accompanied it. Because of these changes, Don Pedro's title was never passed down to his son Juan or to any other member of the Cuevas family. Even though Don Pedro de Cuevas was a minor member of the nobility, he remained a simple farmer all of his life.

A nobleman's house symbolized the wealth, status and continuity of the family. The hidalgo's home was retained and passed down from generation to generation. For this reason, the house of Don Pedro de Cuevas still belongs to the Cuevas family in Algámitas today. It is currently owned by Manuel "Manolo" Sanchez Cuevas, who inherited the house from his mother, Francesca Cuevas Martin, who, in turn, inherited it from her father. Manolo lives in the house with his wife, Mariá, and his mother, Francesca.[61] The house located in the center of town and is one of the five oldest houses in Algámitas. When Juan de Cuevas lived in the village, it had a population of less than 100 people. Today, the population has grown to about 1,400. There are now at least 30 Cuevas families living in Algámitas, a sizeable number for a town so small.

Left: Label from a jar of olives grown in Algámitas, Spain, from Cuevas olive trees. *Photograph by John Cuevas.*

Right: Label from a jar of olive oil produced from Cuevas family olives in Algámitas, Spain. *Photograph by John Cuevas.*

Juan José de Cuevas arrived on the Gulf Coast as a member of the military in 1792, during the Spanish control of the area.[62] King Charles III, who ruled Spain at that time, feared that he was losing control of the Spanish colonies in the New World when he realized they were obtaining goods from other countries. In order to control the situation and force the Spanish colonies to purchase goods from Spain, the king placed restrictions on commerce. This forced the price of European goods to be prohibitive not only in the colonies but also in Spain. To avoid the higher prices and to bring in these much-needed commodities, many of which could not be obtained in Spain, an illegal trade developed between English, French and Dutch smugglers. Smuggling flourished in just about all of the staples: tea, spirits, coffee, tobacco, salt, pepper, gunpowder, precious metals and even enslaved people.[63]

The smugglers began supplying goods to aid the people of Spain, so Juan joined the smugglers for the good of Spain and the well-being of its people. Unfortunately, because of his youth and inexperience, it wasn't long before he was captured by the king's soldiers and taken to a prison in Granada.

At the time, Spain was fighting the British in Florida and the Louisiana Territory. Because of the king's need for soldiers, he offered young Juan a choice. He could remain in prison, or he could join the military and fight in the New World. He chose to become a soldier, knowing he would never see his family again. He was released from prison and joined the troops that

Francesca Cuevas Martin stands in the foyer of the Cuevas home in Algámitas, Spain. Her sister Conception is standing inside the entry gate behind her. *Photograph by John Cuevas.*

had been sent to help the Spanish governor Bernardo de Galvez defeat the British and recapture Fort San Miguel in Pensacola.

After being discharged from the military, Juan first settled on Deer Island around 1793. He is on record as being a shipowner and paying the toll regularly to go through the bridge of Bayou St. John in New Orleans on his trips from Deer Island.[64] On the route to and from New Orleans, Juan would stop over on Cat Island. It was during these visits that he first met the Ladner family and became interested in Nicholas Christian Ladner's daughter Marie Helene.[65] Ladner had received a Spanish land grant for all of Cat Island in 1781.[66] Several people were using the islands in the Mississippi Sound as cattle pasturage at that time.[67] In 1785, Ladner built the old house on Cat Island that would eventually become known as the old Cuevas homestead.[68]

In 1795, about two years after arriving on the coast, Juan de Cuevas married Marie Ladner, and they made their home on Deer Island, where Juan was living.[69] Due to declining health and the prospects of a more comfortable life on the mainland, Nicholas petitioned Governor Miró for

The old Cuevas homestead on Cat Island. *Courtesy of the John Cuevas collection.*

land at what is now Long Beach. On June 3, 1788, just two weeks after his request, Spain granted him the land.[70]

After clearing the land, Nicholas began constructing the new Ladner home. A chimney was placed at each gable end of the house, approximately forty feet apart. These chimneys were tall and could be seen from the vessels that passed in the open waters of the gulf. The high-profile visibility of the chimneys eventually gave the Ladner's home the landmark name "The Chimneys."[71] The house was finished around 1801.

It is not clear when Nicholas Ladner died, but it was around 1805, leaving Cat Island and the Chimneys to his widow, Marianne.[72] After Ladner passed away, Juan and Marie had moved back and forth between their home on Deer Island and the Ladner home on Cat Island to take care of Marie's mother. Since the Cuevas family had made the Ladner house their second home, Juan asked his mother-in-law to sell him the island once she had permanently settled on the mainland. On July 24, 1810, Juan purchased Cat Island from Marie's mother for the sum of $160.[73] Juan and Marie moved into the old Ladner home on Cat Island after the purchase of the island.

When the Cuevas family moved over to Cat Island, the population along the coast was very sparse. According to a report issued on May 1, 1804, by Ephraim Kirby, the special commissioner on Spanish boundary, there were only forty-eight families living between Mobile Bay and the Pearl River.[74] Six years later, an anonymous traveler passing through counted only twelve families in Biloxi, with only ten to fifteen families living at Bay of St. Louis, and in Pass Christian, there were four or five. The tax rolls show that only eight families were living in Long Beach (then known as "The Chimneys"). In 1810, the population of New Orleans was 24,550, while the population of Mobile had dwindled to only 300.[75]

The story that has been passed down for generations began on December 8, 1814, when the Cuevas family awoke to find an array of fifty large warships stretched out in the gulf, practically on the family's doorstep. The British fleet was preparing to strike a surprise blow to the city of New Orleans. When the British discovered Juan and the Cuevas family on Cat Island, they captured the family, forcing Juan to guide the ships through the tricky marshes into the city. Reluctantly, he agreed to help his captors, although he never had any intention of helping the British. He told the officers he would steer them up the mouth of the Mississippi River. Although Juan made the enemy believe he was showing the way, he actually led the big ships into the mouth of the Pearl River. When the large boats got stuck in the shallow water, he was able to escape. He borrowed a pirogue from friendly Natives nearby and rowed to the Rigolettes, where he alerted the guards that the British were about to attack.

With the information that Juan provided, General Jackson was able to overpower the British in the most decisive victory of the War of 1812. The beaten British troops limped back to their base near Ship Island and released Juan's family before sailing away.[76] Although Andrew Jackson and Jean Lafitte have both gone down in history as heroes in the Battle of New Orleans, according to legend, it was Juan de Cuevas who actually fired the first shots against the invading British.[77]

While the story of Juan de Cuevas and the Battle of New Orleans is mostly fictional, Juan was a certified hero when he captured two pirates in July 1820 near his home on Cat Island.[78] The two men, John Baker and Martin Hogan, had taken over a boat that was headed for New Orleans with a large load of silks from France. Juan overpowered the two men and then rowed to New Orleans to inform the boat's owners about the piracy. The two were tried, convicted of piracy and sentenced to hang.

For his heroic capture of the two pirates in the gulf, Juan de Cuevas was given official recognition by the state of Mississippi and a cash reward. The capture of the two pirates is not a legend—it is a fact. And for this reason, Juan de Cuevas can rightfully be called the "Hero of Cat Island."

Juan de Cuevas died on September 24, 1849, at the age of eighty-seven. His obituary appeared in the *Daily Picayune* on September 27, 1849. It was the only burial notice in the paper that was written in three languages: French, English and his native Spanish.[79]

A customary wake was held for Juan at his home on the island. The funeral for Juan was typical for the time. There was a period of full mourning that lasted six months, during which time, Marie and the children wore traditional black Creole mourning clothes. She also wore a small flat bonnet with a long black veil called a calotte. The men wore black ties and black hat bands. Some wore black crepe around their arms. After the first six-month period, a widow could alter her mourning clothes by edging her black dress with white collars and cuffs.[80] Funeral homes did not exist, so wakes were normally held in the homes of the deceased. Being in the home, it was not unusual for the body to be positioned comfortably on a couch in the living room to give an appearance that the deceased was still with the family.[81]

People believed that the spirit of the dead stayed around the house for three days, during which time, the mourners kept a traditional vigil around the clock. It was the practice at that time that a body should never be left alone between the time of death and final burial. The reason for this was more precautionary than religious. Innocent people feared the possibility of being buried alive. Some diseases, such as yellow fever, produced symptoms that often made it difficult to say with certainty that the person was actually dead. Medicine was not sophisticated enough in those days to provide scientific proof. Embalming was not used until after the Civil War. President Lincoln advocated for embalming, as it allowed the Union dead enough time to be shipped back to their hometowns for appropriate burials during the war.[82]

Juan was originally buried on Cat Island until a family vault was built for him in the Old Biloxi Cemetery.[83]

JOSEPH ROBERT DAVIS: NEPHEW OF CONFEDERATE PRESIDENT JEFFERSON DAVIS

James Robert Davis, the nephew of Confederate president Jefferson Davis (June 3, 1808–December 6, 1889), was born in Woodville, Mississippi, on January 12, 1825. He received his law degree from Miami University in Oxford, Ohio. He began his law practice in Madison County, Mississippi, before running for the Mississippi State Senate. He was elected to the senate in 1860.[84]

Joseph Robert Davis. *Photograph by Chris Cahill.*

James joined the militia as a captain without any previous military training. He was promoted almost immediately to the rank of lieutenant-colonel of the Tenth Regiment, Mississippi Volunteers, but he never saw much combat. He was assigned to the staff of his uncle President Jeff Davis, serving as an aide de camp. On August 21, 1862, he was promoted again, this time, to full colonel of the cavalry. He then now living in the Confederate White House with President Davis and touring the South with his uncle. He visited the troops and would write reports about the military.[85]

On September 15, 1862, when James was further promoted to the rank of brigadier-general there was loud opposition to his appointment, charging that it was nepotism. At first, the Confederate senate rejected the promotion, but only five days later, the body reversed its decision. James Davis's promotion was finally approved by a vote of thirteen to six. Georgia senator Benjamin Harvey Hill (September 14, 1823–August 16, 1882) had arranged to have the senate reconsider the vote, resulting in an immediate reversal of their original decision. It was believed by many to have been a political payoff to Senator Hill.

James Davis was assigned to a brigade in the Army of Northern Virginia under General Henry Heath (December 16, 1825–September 27, 1899), leading it through some of the most hostile battles of the war. He also fought at Gettysburg, where his troops suffered heavy casualties on the first day of the battle. On the third day, his brigade supported Major-General George Edward Pickett (January 16, 1825–July 30, 1875) in the Wilderness Campaign and at the Siege of Petersburg.[86]

Brigadier-General Joseph R. Davis returned to the Mississippi Gulf Coast to resume practicing law after being paroled at Appomattox on April 9, 1865, by General Ulysses S. Grant (1822–1885). In 1878, he divorced his wife, Frances H. Peyton Davis, after being married for thirty years. A year later, he married Margaret Cary Green, with whom he went on to have three children.[87]

Joseph R. Davis died in Biloxi on September 15, 1896, at the age of eighty-one.[88]

JEAN CHEVALIER DELAUNEY: CREATED THE FIRST PERMANENT FREE LIBRARY IN THE STATE OF MISSISSIPPI

Jean Chevalier Delauney was born on December 23, 1780, in Bordeaux, France, just nine years before the start of the French Revolution. This was a period in which the centuries-old institutions in France were being completely discarded and redesigned. The turmoil was the result of King Louis XVI's extravagant spending in the colonies, along with poor tax practices in the country. This left France near bankruptcy. Not only had the king imposed a heavy land tax on the people to ease the financial crisis, but the privileged classes were exempt. Unrest among the French people was kindled not only by the irresponsible governing of King Louis XVI but also by two decades of draughts resulting in poor harvest, disease and bread prices so high that the peasants and the urban poor could not afford bread. Rioting, looting and general unrest were the desperate expressions of resentment. The cries for help were met by derision, as

Jean Chevalier Delauney. *Photograph by Chris Cahill.*

Marie Antoinette, the wife of the king made her infamous statement that if the people couldn't have bread, "let them eat cake."[89]

Jean's father, Pierre Delauney, hoping to avoid the political turmoil in France, applied for a passport to the United States, settling in Philadelphia, Pennsylvania. Jean, whose mother had died at the age of thirty when Jean was only four years old, was left in the care of his aged aunt Marie Dufour. Marie raised Jean and his older brother, Robert. On October 29, 1796, after living in the United States for three years, Pierre was granted American citizenship. Working for various shipping companies, he was able to finally earn enough money to send for his oldest son. When in the states, Robert was sent to boarding school in Connecticut. The plan was to bring Jean over as soon as he could afford it, but Jean grew impatient and made the move on his own, arriving around 1801.[90]

In 1808, Pierre remarried and had a son, Charles. Four years later, Jean's brother Robert died. Sometime around 1815, Jean married Elizabeth Ireland and had three children: Robert, Catherine Elizabeth and Therese. In 1819, he moved with his family from Philadelphia to New Orleans, after which the couple had two more children: Pierre Henri and Louise Josephine. While in New Orleans, Jean worked as a carpenter. His five children attended school in the city.

In 1820, Jean visited Biloxi for the first time and fell in love with the Gulf Coast. Wishing to one day live there, he purchased property on the beachfront between Lameuse Street and Rue Magnolia. The land went from the beach all the way to Back Bay Biloxi. After building a summer home on the site, he and his family visited the coast often.[91]

In 1823, Jean's wife, Elizabeth, died in New Orleans. Their youngest child was only a year old at the time. On March 5, 1829, Jean married his second wife, Adele Ladner. Jean and Adele had eight children. Adele was the daughter of Joseph Nicholas Ladner and Rosalie Fayard (circa 1780–circa 1855). Rosalie's sister was Margarite Fayard.[92] They were the daughters of Jean Baptiste Fayard II and Angelique Ladner, members of two of the coast's oldest families. Margarite was married to Louis-Francois Arbau Caillavet, the son of Louis Caillavet (see biography).

By 1835, Jean and his family had moved permanently from New Orleans to Biloxi, where Jean began buying land. He purchased and ran a hotel and made a good living working as a notary public, since he and Louis Caillavet were among the only men on the coast who could read or write. He also managed his properties, renting out cottages to summer tourists. He embarked on an aggressive advertising campaign in the New

Orleans paper, hoping to attract wealthy vacationers to Biloxi and the Gulf Coast.[93]

In 1905, one of Jean Delauney's cottages became the first permanent free library in the state of Mississippi. The building, known as the Creole Cottage, is still in the city. It has survived numerous hurricanes and remains in the city of Biloxi today.

Jean Chevalier Delauney died in 1862 and was buried in the Old Biloxi Cemetery. Delauney Street in Biloxi is named after Jean Delauney and his family.

WILLIAM K.M. DUKATE: ONE OF THE FATHERS OF BILOXI'S SEAFOOD INDUSTRY

K.M. DuKate (1852–1916) is considered one of the fathers of the seafood industry in Biloxi, as he worked during the time when Biloxi became known as the "seafood capital of the world."[94]

Born in Fredericksburg, Indiana, in 1852, DuKate came to the Gulf Coast in the 1870s, working for the L&N Railroad as a telegraph operator. On April 27, 1878, he married a local girl, Linda Rose Lienhard (1859–1939), the daughter of Peter J. Lienhard (1812–1873), a Swiss immigrant, and Malinda B. Seaman (1826–1890). The couple had six children: Elbert, Eula, Vera Linda, Leola, Irma and Buela.

In 1881, DuKate and four other businessmen built a seafood cannery on the Back Bay of Biloxi. William K.M. DuKate, along with F. William Elmer (1847–1926), William Gorenflo (1844–1932) and James Maycock (1826–1892), seeing and opportunity in an untapped seafood industry, came together to form Lopez, Elmer and Company for the purpose of canning seafood. The men realized they were novices in the business and needed to improve their knowledge of the operation. William DuKate was selected to travel to Baltimore, where the seafood processing business was already booming. DuKate studied their methods and was able to implement what he had learned when he returned to Biloxi. One of the most important things he discovered was their use of immigrant workers on a seasonal basis. The company immediately began advertising for part-time employees. Yugoslavian, Austrian, Polish and Acadian immigrants poured into Biloxi to fill the positions. The timing was right, and the small business was profitable from the start.[95]

William K.M. Dukate. *Photograph by Chris Cahill.*

By December 1881, the company had employed over one hundred men and boys. The positions included forty-four machine operators, forty-five men manning fifteen boats and twenty-plus canners and wharf men.[96]

On March 23, 1883, the Biloxi Canning Company was incorporated. With the creation of the new corporation, the old Lopez, Elmer and Company dissolved, and the original founders went on to form their own companies. The seafood packing industry was growing so swiftly that it wasn't long before the Barataria Canning Company, Lopez & DuKate, William Gorenflo & Company, E.C. Joullian & Company, J.T. Maybury and Dunbar's Sons & Company were in fierce competition.

On October 12, 1894, a large fire ravaged several properties in downtown Biloxi, including the DuKate residence and $3,000 worth of pottery by the "Mad Potter," George Ohr.[97] After the fire, William DuKate built a magnificent new residence at a cost of $4,500 on the corner of Pass Christian Street (Howard Avenue) and Magnolia Street.[98]

The growth of the Gulf Coast fishing industry continued to expand at such a rapid pace that by 1902, the canning factories in Biloxi ranked second in America for the canning of oysters.[99] In that same year, Lopez & DuKate expanded into Louisiana, building a large oyster cannery, house, store, warehouse and camp at the Rigolets.

In December 1922, the DuKate mansion was sold to a group of descendants of Lazarus Lopez (1850–1903), Edward L. Brady (1874–1939), Erena Lopez Brady (1885–1940) and Teresa Lopez Folkes (1873–1951). The home was demolished in July 1923 to make way for a five-story, one-hundred-room hotel for a cost of $60,000. The new hotel was to be called the Avelez Hotel, and it was to feature modern furniture and a bathroom in every room.[100] The name of the hotel came from the hometown of Lazarus Lopez, who was born in Aviles, Asturias Province, Northwestern Spain in October 1850.[101]

Both William DuKate and his wife, Linda, were very active in the Biloxi community. William DuKate was a member of the Biloxi School Board, the board of trustees of the Bank of Biloxi (now Peoples Bank) and several other boards and committees. A much-needed school on the Back Bay called the Back Bay Ward School was built with funds provided by William K.M. DuKate.[102]

In addition to his other civic contributions, William DuKate built a modern, state-of-the-art opera house and performing arts center. The house that he gave to his daughter Vera in 1904 for her wedding was later donated to the city of Biloxi and now serves as Biloxi's visitor's center.

William K.M. DuKate died in 1916 and was buried in the Old Biloxi Cemetery.

FREDRICK WILLIAM ELMER: CREDITED WITH CREATING BEACH BOULEVARD (HIGHWAY 90), THREE-TERM MAYOR OF BILOXI

The Elmer family had a great effect on the city of Biloxi and the entire Gulf Coast. Fredrick William Elmer, the once-mayor of Biloxi, is credited with changing a cow trail along the gulf into what would become Beach Boulevard (Highway 90). He was successful in getting it grated and covered with oyster shells. The road became imminently important during the time when Biloxi was becoming known as the "Riviera of the United States."[103]

His brother Augustus Elmer created the Elmer Candy Company of New Orleans, famous for its iconic candy bars, Heavenly Hash and Gold Brick Eggs. Easter would not be the same without these luscious seasonal chocolate bars.

Frederick William Elmer was born in Biloxi on January 23, 1847. Frederick married Elizabeth Carson Maycock (1850–1905) in May 1871. She was the daughter of Captain James Maycock (1825–1892) and Mary Emily Carson (1827–1900). Captain Maycock, who was born in Hull,

Elmer family. *Photograph by Chris Cahill.*

Yorkshire, England, in 1825, had arrived in Biloxi in 1839, when he was only fourteen years old. Although he came with very little money, Captain Jack proved to be an able businessman and soon had accumulated a respectable amount of wealth. He joined his son-in-law, Frederick W. Elmer, and three other men, Lazaro Lopez, William K.M. DuKate and William Gorenflo, to form a seafood canning business called Lopez, Elmer and Company. The five men are considered to be the fathers of the then-burgeoning seafood industry in Biloxi.[104]

As he became more successful in business, Frederick Elmer was called to civic duty by first serving as a supervisor of Harrison County for over twenty years. After his stint as supervisor, he served as an alderman of Ward 2 in Biloxi and was finally elected mayor of Biloxi for three terms, beginning on January 6, 1891.

In October 1904, Mayor Elmer and his wife, Elizabeth, who had been living at 120 Water Street, began the construction on their dream home. The two-story, 2,500-square-foot home was situated on a 1.37-acre lot at Magnolia and Front Beach (now Highway 90). When finished, it would cost between $3,000 and $4,000, a considerable sum for that time.[105] Unfortunately, Elizabeth Elmer did not live to see her dream home completed.[106] She had suffered with heart disease for the last two years of her life, and she died suddenly on January 21, 1905, when she was only fifty-four years old. The funeral services for Elizabeth were conducted at the family home on Water Street before the burial in the Old Biloxi Cemetery. Her father, Captain James Maycock, who had died on March 19, 1892, was also buried in the Biloxi Cemetery.

She and her husband were devoted members of the Episcopal Church of the Redeemer. Her father, Captain James Maycock, was one of the original members of the vestry, a group of parishioners in an Episcopal parish who are elected to administer the secular affairs of the parish. The Elmer and Maycock families often attended services with their friends President and Mrs. Jefferson Davis and the Davis family.

William Fredrick Elmer passed away on December 23, 1926. He was buried with his wife in the Old Biloxi Cemetery. The *Daily Herald* was quoted as saying, "One of the most useful citizens that Biloxi has ever produced has passed from this life."

JOHN R. GUILHOT: THE "HERMIT OF DEER ISLAND"

On a hot, sultry evening in July 1899, in Dunsmore, Pennsylvania, a small town near Scranton, two men were lurking about in the shadows. One man carried a pipe bomb loaded with deadly explosives; both were armed with pistols. A watchful neighbor alerted the police of their suspicious behavior. According to the *Scranton Tribune*, two officers, Henry Snyder and Patrick Kays, confronted the suspects in the front yard of one of the town's homes. The men dropped the pipe bomb and fired at the officers before fleeing the scene. Both officers were wounded. Although one was seriously injured, both survived and reported that the two suspects were Frenchmen who spoke in broken English. The men were able to escape, but a $500 reward was offered for their capture.[107]

In 1900, a Montreal detective was sitting at a bar in Canada when he overheard two Frenchmen bragging about shooting two policemen in Pennsylvania. The superintendent of police in Montreal contacted Pennsylvania authorities, and the two men were arrested. The names they gave to the authorities were Auguste Morel and Antoine Robert; the men readily confessed to the crime. The two were extradited back to Pennsylvania, where they were sentenced to five years in Eastern State Penitentiary. Their real names were discovered to be Jean Guilhot (pronounced Gee-O) and Francis Merlier. It was learned that Jean Guilhot was born in France on October 27, 1877. He arrived in in the United States in 1898 at the age of twenty-one. It is not clear whether he and Merlier came to this country together, but within a year, they had teamed up to carry out an act of terrorism.[108]

John R. Guilhot. *Photograph by Chris Cahill.*

Eastern State Penitentiary is a former prison located in Philadelphia, Pennsylvania.[109] It was the first prison to emphasize reform rather than punishment.[110] When it was built in 1829, it was the largest and most expensive public building ever built at that time.[111] It was closed in 1971 and is now a National Historic Landmark that is operated as a museum.[112]

Research assistant E.W. Suarez of the Biloxi Local History and Genealogy Department discovered an Associated Press report from November 1900 that named Francois Merlier, Guilhot's accomplice, as having connections to an anarchist gang that had been plotting to kill President William McKinley (January 29, 1843–September 14, 1901). While the men were still incarcerated, a twenty-eight-year-old anarchist named Leon Czolgosz from Poland shot President McKinley, who later died from the wound. Suarez said the documents confirmed that Jean Guilhot was an early domestic terrorist.[113]

In 1904, after serving only four years of their sentences, the men were released early due to good behavior. Census records and other documents indicate they stayed together for a while. After about three years, the men drifted apart, and Jean Guilhot ended up in Key West, Florida. There, he met his first wife, Charlotte. They were married in 1907. Twenty years later, they separated, and in the early 1920s, Jean made his way to Biloxi, where he began living on Deer Island. While on the coast, he met and married Pauline Lemien Riel. Pauline was born in Chicago, Illinois, in April 1866 and had been living in Biloxi for about ten years before she and Jean were married.

Reports indicate that Jean worked as a barber, and at one time, it is said he grew oysters on Deer Island in a small oyster plant. On December 14, 1933, Pauline died, leaving Jean alone with his dogs on the island. He grew increasingly introverted, and while he was very friendly, he became even more secluded. Fourteen years after his wife's death, the coast was hit by the hurricane of 1947. All attempts to save Jean from the powerful storm were unsuccessful. He refused to go to the safety of a shelter on the mainland; instead, he climbed one of the high trees on the island, determined to ride out the storm. Miraculously, he survived, but his small shack was destroyed. After the trauma of the hurricane, he became even more reclusive.

As the years went by, Jean became somewhat of a dichotomous figure; on the one hand, he seemed to shun any attention, while at the same time, it was obvious that he invited it. Mr. Louis Gorenflo, who ran a tour boat called the *Sailfish*, felt compassion for the man, and over time, the two became good friends. As Jean grew older, he could no longer row the distance to the mainland for supplies. Gorenflo would deliver groceries to him when he needed them. Louis would also take a newspaper to Jean and whatever small amount of mail he received. He would leave it tied to a pine tree stump out in the gulf near the island. Jean enjoyed rowing out to meet the *Sailfish* and serenading the passengers with French folk songs. He supported himself with the change the tourists would throw to him. This was great for Jean, but it was also an added attraction for Gornflo's tour business. The people loved to see the crusty old Frenchman and have him entertain them with his

French folk songs. He became so popular that Gorenflo even used him in his advertising, placing a picture of the grisly old "hermit" on all of his posters.

As time went by, Jean tired of entertaining, so he rigged a pulley and rope system attached to the pine tree with a cup for retrieving his mail. He never left the island and would only wave as the *Sailfish* sailed by with its passengers.

Jean Guilhot died on May 27, 1959.[114] So much of his story is steeped in mystery and legend that it is difficult to separate what is true and what is not. Although he is known as the "hermit of Deer Island," he was, in fact, hardly a hermit. He had a great personality and loved telling his stories to anyone who would listen.

Walter Henry "Skeet" Hunt: Created the Isle of Caprice, a Gambling Paradise in the Gulf, the "Father of the Mardi Gras" in Biloxi

Walter Henry "Skeet" Hunt, born in Biloxi on January 11, 1891, became known as the "Father of the Mardi Gras."

In 1892, Skeeter Hunt, as he was called in those days, was four years old when a Mardi Gras parade of sorts passed in front of his house. Although not an official Mardi Gras parade, it had been organized as such by the volunteer fire departments in Biloxi. While it was not like the parades we know today, with all of their glitz and glamour, there were still many flashy elements. King Rex officially landed in a boat at the Main Street dock, along with his queen and some simple floats. There were also flambeaux carriers that would later become an important part of the parades. Little Skeeter Hunt was captivated by the magic of Mardi Gras that he witnessed that day. This experience was the catalyst that led to a permanent Mardi Gras celebration in Biloxi, a celebration that would grow to include all of the cities on the Gulf Coast.[115]

In 1908, the first official Mardi Gras parade was held. The parade was led by the Boeuf Gras, or "the fatted bull." The animal was a white bull decorated with gilded horns. Following the bull were the grand marshal, the mayor and city officials, 17 floats, the newly formed *Herald* newspaper band and 150 flambeau carriers.

The custom of the Boeuf Gras has been associated with the pre-Lenten season going back to the Middle Ages. The symbol represents the last beef

Walter Skeet Hunt. *Photograph by Chris Cahill.*

eaten before the start of Lent. A live bull decorated with garlands of flowers marched in the Mardi Gras parade in New Orleans from 1871 to 1900. The bull disappeared from the parades for some reason after 1900 and didn't reappear until 1959. When Boeuf Gras was revived, a live bull was not used; instead, the live animal was substituted with a more decorative papier-mâché version.[116]

In 1916, the Biloxi Carnival and Literary Association was formed with the principals being Mayor Edward Glennan (1854–1933), W.H. "Skeet" Hunt, C.J. Keller, J.V. Hagan and Charles Rushing. The original purpose of the organization was to create an annual street festival using colorfully decorated floats representing figures from various historic events to promote the study of literature, particularly Greek mythology. Because of this group, Mardi Gras in Biloxi became an annual event. It was exclusive to Biloxi until 1929, when other coastal cities were invited to participate. By 1949, the name of the organization had been changed to the Gulf Coast Carnival Association.

Skeet Hunt was actively involved from the beginning, serving as grand marshal and parade chairman for forty-four years. In addition, he served in other positions within the group. In 1950, he became the general manager of the carnival association and the parade chairman. In 1953, he became the first captain of the carnival association, serving in that position until 1971.[117]

On July 4, 1924, Colonel Jack R. Apperson opened his Buena Vista Hotel. It had been designed by architect Carl Matthes in a mission-style, stucco design. This five-story, U-shaped building featured two hundred guest rooms facing the beach road (later Highway 90), overlooking the Mississippi Sound. In the 1920s, the Mississippi Gulf Coast was beginning to attract many tourists who were seeking a warmer climate and fun on the water. Apperson and others in the business community were seeking ways to attract new visitors to the coast. Skeet Hunt, an ambitious young businessman who was still in his twenties, shared the desire to find something special to attract tourists to the area.

When Hunt became aware of Dog Island, a small three-mile-long island off the coast of Biloxi between Horn and Ship Island, he realized he had found just the thing the coast needed. Skeet purchased Dog Island from an attorney, paying him $183.75. Joining with fellow Biloxi entrepreneurs, Arbeau Caillavet and Colonel Jack Apperson, the men pooled their resources and creative imaginations to create a beautiful destination.

As John Cuevas describes it in his book *Cat Island* (McFarland, 2011), "Dog Key, positioned directly south of the Buena Vista, was perfect for their needs. With windswept dunes and white sandy beaches, it was the ideal location to create a gambling paradise in the gulf, a 'Monte Carlo of the South.'" Since it was beyond the twelve-mile limit allowed by international law, the state would have no authority to impose any kinds of restrictions on gambling or alcohol. Dog Key was romantically renamed the "Isle of Caprice" to signify its carefree character. The current Biloxi casino Isle of Capri derived its name from this popular resort.

The 487-acre island was approximately three miles long and one-quarter mile wide. Colonel Jack built two large buildings for the resort. One housed the gambling facilities and a dance floor, while the other housed a dressing room for swimmers. In addition, he built ten rental cabins that were nestled among the sand dunes, with a boardwalk connecting all of the buildings. A 150-foot-long pier was constructed on the north side of the island opposite the coast with an artesian well that had been dug at the entrance to provide fresh water to the guests. An old boat named *Hercules* was purchased and renamed the *Non-Pareil*, which means "none like it." The vessel made four trips daily from the coast to the island landing.

The daily herald reported on July 4, 1925, that the Isle of Caprice would open the next day, on July 5. Tourists from as far away as Illinois boarded boats from piers at the Buena Vista Hotel and Cuevas Avenue in Biloxi to enjoy swimming, dancing and gambling at the new resort. Skeet Hunt, ever the promoter, created a marathon swimming race from the mainland to the island. He also provided big band entertainment to the many happy patrons who danced and gambled until the last boat left at 4:00 a.m.

In 1926, a New Orleans newspaper reported:

> *There were soft, thick carpets on the floor and a general atmosphere of quiet luxury. Divans along the wall were tapestried and deep cushioned, mahogany-colored and cane-bottom stools were on hand for the gamblers. A roulette table, two craps tables, a bird cage and a Faro layout comprised the paraphernalia that made the place spin. A busy money changer (the one in the cap) with a capacious bankroll walked about, and each table was operated by a croupier plentifully supplied with chips and funds.*

The future seemed bright until a hurricane struck and split the small island in two. Not only that, but the island's beautiful sea oats had been harvested by so many souvenir seekers that the island began to wash away. There was a double blow, as the Great Depression of the 1930s took away people's fun money. Times were tough, and the Isle of Caprice was struggling. In 1931, a fire of unknown origin destroyed much of the buildings on the island, and with little ado, Caprice was swallowed up by the sea. For years, the only evidence of the Isle of Caprice was a pipe sticking out of the gulf that spewed artesian water from a well that once provided water on the island. Fishermen would stop and take a swig from the pipe of what the *Daily Herald* called "sweet water." The pipe has long since disappeared beneath the surface of the gulf like the island itself.

Facing financial disaster, Skeet Hunt accepted a job with the U.S. Capitol Police in Washington, D.C., with the help of U.S. senator Pat Harrison (August 29, 1881–June 22, 1941). While serving with the police, Hunt continued his duties with the Mardi Gras organization. In 1945, he was diagnosed with a terminal illness. Always an entrepreneur, he didn't let the disease slow him down. He started a restaurant in Biloxi called Skeet's Place, which featured quality gulf seafood.[118] During that time, he patented a process of packing and shipping frozen food all over the United States. Unfortunately, tragedy struck again when the 1947 hurricane destroyed his plant at the foot of the Biloxi/Ocean Springs Bridge. In 1959, he retired from the Capitol Police in Washington, D.C., and on January 13, 1961, at the age of seventy-three, Walter Skeet succumbed to cancer, ending his colorful life. His wife, Rose, who was also from Biloxi, died on July 9, 1985, at the age of ninety-four. They were both buried in the Old Biloxi Cemetery.

JOSEPH HENRY "DINKY" LAMAS: KILLED BY A BEAR IN THE NAVAL RESERVE PARK ZOO

Joseph "Dinky" Lamas was born in Biloxi on February 11, 1897. He was not a civic leader, he was not a war hero, he was not doctor or scientist, and during his short life, he had accomplished very little of importance. So, why is he included in our list of special people buried in the Old Biloxi Cemetery? It was not how he lived that made him special—it was the way he died.

Many may not remember the Naval Reserve Park Zoo that once existed on Back Bay Biloxi. It opened around 1928 and closed sometime around 1934. The park was maintained by the naval reserve and provided access to Back Bay for boating, fishing and other water sports. It also provided green space for families in the surrounding neighborhoods to picnic and relax in the serenity of the large oak trees. The park also featured a small zoo containing a handful of common animals and exotic birds, like peacocks.

Dinky Lamas and his family lived at the Naval Reserve Park. His father, Rudolph Lamas, was born in 1876 in Pascagoula. He was well known on the coast and was an expert fisherman and hunter. He and Dinky loved the animals. He had previously been in the seafood industry and had operated a very popular lunchroom on East Beach.

Dinky Lamas met his wife, Gladys Purcell from Biloxi, and they were married on August 24, 1924, when Dinky was twenty-seven years old and she was eighteen.[119] Dinky and Gladys looked after the animals at the zoo. They made sure that the animals were fed properly and had plenty of water to survive the hot, steamy weather of the coast. They treated the animals like they were family pets.

On October 29, 1931, Dinky Lamas entered the cage of a three-year-old black bear that was the zoo's biggest attraction. He had brought the bear's food, as he had done every day since the bear had arrived. As he turned to leave the cage, something snapped in the bear, and Lamas was attacked viciously from behind. His wife, Gladys, was nearby and heard her husband's screams. Putting her own life at risk, she rushed into the cage, fighting back the bear as Dinky pulled himself to safety.[120]

Dinky was rushed to the hospital and was treated for his injuries. His wife had done everything she could to save his life, but the effort was to no avail. During the night, a bad infection set in, and Joseph Dinky Lamas died around midnight on October 30, 1931.

Joseph Henry "Dinky" Lamas. *Photograph by Chris Cahill.*

The bear was not only killed, but it was also put on display for the curious public to see. There was an extensive investigation of the incident to determine how such an accident could have occurred. The whole tragedy and the heroic action that Gladys took by entering the bear's cage to save her husband's life attracted more attention than any other news item for months on the coast.

Dinky's parents, Rudolph and Catherine Coleman, were devastated, but they also knew the risk involved in caring for wild animals. Since the animals that were left needed attention, Dinky's father, Rudolph, stepped in to replace him. Rudolph served as the director of the zoo for seven years after that. The zoo closed around 1934, probably due to the adverse publicity that Dinky's death caused. At the time of its closing, only a few peacocks remained at the zoo.[121] Rudolph Lamas died on May 29, 1938, at the age of sixty-two. He had been ill for about five years, but he was terminally ill for only a short time before his death.[122]

Eight years after his death, Dinky's widow, Gladys, married Dinky's brother Ralph (December 21, 1902–March 10, 1982), who everyone called "Son." Gladys died on November 14, 1979, at the age of seventy-three.[123]

LAZARO "LAZ" LOPEZ: ONE OF THE FATHERS OF BILOXI'S SEAFOOD INDUSTRY

Lazaro "Laz" Lopez was born on October 11, 1850, in Aviles, Asturias Province, Northwestern Spain. He is considered one of the fathers of the seafood industry in Biloxi during the time when Biloxi was known as the "seafood capital of the world."[124]

Laz Lopez was from a good family, but even the nobility at that time could not read or write. He was taught a basic education at home before leaving Spain in 1863. He was only thirteen years old when he headed to Cuba. He then traveled to Texas before moving to Biloxi to settle. He spoke almost no English and had almost no money. Since he had no formal training, he took whatever work he could find. He went to work for Joseph Garcia (1828–circa 1870), who owned and operated a coffee house in Biloxi. Garcia, also from Spain, allowed Laz to live with him. Later, Laz worked as a bartender in a bar run by Andrew Nugarre (1840–1870), another Spaniard living in Biloxi.[125] In 1871, Laz met Julia Dulion of Biloxi, and on August 19 of that year, they were married. Julia was the daughter of a French immigrant named Arnaud Michel Dulion (1830–1870). Her mother, Mary Ann Keegan (1832–1890), was a native of Ireland. Laz and Julia had ten children: Josephine Mary Angeline (1872–1892), Teresa (1873–1951), Clara (1875–1895), Lazaro T. (1877–1918), Arnaud (1880–1948), Erena (1885–1940), Julius M. (1886–1958), Juanita Olivia (1890–1891), Rowena Maria (1895–1986) and Noreta Julia (1896–1960).[126]

In a few years, Laz was able to open a grocery store. It was located at the corner of Pass Christian Road (later named Howard Avenue) and Lameuse Street. As his business grew, he moved down the road to a larger location at the corner of Reynoir Street and Pass Christian Road.

In 1881, Laz Lopez and four other Biloxi businessmen invested a total of $8,000 to form a company for canning oysters. Laz, along with F.W. Elmer, W.K.M. Dukate, James Maycock and William Gorenflo, opened Lopez, Elmer & Company Seafood Plant, the first oyster packing enterprise in Biloxi. The company canned oysters and shrimp and offered raw oysters in bulk.[127] The company later became known as the Biloxi Canning Company.

Seafood canning was an entirely new enterprise for these men. In order to learn the business, William K.M. DuKate was selected by the group to travel to Baltimore to study the packing industry there that was already well established. While he was in Baltimore, DuKate also purchased the necessary machinery for their new enterprise.[128]

Lazaro Lopez. *Photograph by Chris Cahill.*

In 1884, Lazaro Lopez and William DuKate resigned from the Biloxi Canning Company and started a company called the Lopez, Dunbar's Sons & Company. Later, the name was changed to Lopez and DuKate. By 1895, the company had become the second largest oyster canning plant in the United States. The company utilized a newly patented muslin bag that ensured a good product. It sold its shrimp under several different labels: "Dunbar Standard," "Deer Head," "Lion's Head" and "Pelicans" brands.[129]

In addition to his work managing the canning companies, Laz Lopez was also a founder of the Biloxi branch of the Inter-State Building & Loan Association of Columbus, Georgia. The Inter-State Building & Loan Association was founded in December 1889.[130] Three years later, on December 26, 1892, the Bank of Biloxi was incorporated.[131] The first officers of the Bank of Biloxi were C.F. Theobald, president; Lazaro Lopez, vice president; and E.J. Buck, cashier.[132]

On June 4, 1900, Lazaro's daughter Teresa married the prominent Biloxi doctor Hyman McMackin Folkes (October 6, 1871–May 1, 1926). The young couple began living in a house they called Waverly near Dr. Folkes's Howard Avenue office, not too far from the Lopez family home. In November of that year, a great fire swept through Biloxi, destroying much of the downtown area, including the Lopez home. In 1901, the Folkeses began planning a new home. With the fire in mind, they purchased land outside of the city on Rodenburg Avenue, next to the beach. The house was completed in 1905 at a cost of $14,000. The house they named Gunston Hall had a two-story portico with four ionic columns across the front in the Neoclassical Revival style (1895–1950) that was popular with homes along the coast at that time.

On May 1, 1926, Dr. Folkes died. In 1939, Teresa built a new home closer to town and sold Gunston Hall to Mr. and Mrs. Harry Allen Wendt. Mr. Wendt was killed in World War II, and Mrs. Wendt sold the house in 1966 to A. Jake and John Mladinich. The Mladinich brothers converted the home into the now-popular White Pillars Restaurant.[133]

On September 25, 1902, Lazaro "Laz" Lopez died in Rome, Italy, from acute inflammation of the kidneys and dysentery while on a pleasure trip to Europe. Accompanying him on the trip were his wife, Julia, and four of his children: Erena, Rowena, Noretta and Julius. When he had left Biloxi a few weeks before, there was no indication that he would become ill.[134]

The body of Laz Lopez arrived by train in Biloxi on October 17, 1903. His funeral was held on Monday, October 20, at 10:00 a.m. at the Biloxi Church of the Nativity of the Blessed Virgin Mary. A high requiem mass was celebrated in his honor by father Alphonse Kettels. The pall bearers and honorary pallbearers read like a who's who of Biloxi's business and political community. The pallbearers were Phil Wachenfeld, Joseph Arguelles, John Wentzell, Joseph Rusk, August "Gus" Barthes and D.M. McCarroll. Serving as honorary pallbearers were W.K.M. Dukate, William F. Gorenflo Sr., Captain John Walker, John C. Bradford, T.J. Rosell, William Buck, Florian Seal, George W. Young, Aristede Hopkins, George W. Grayson, John E. Morrison and Walter A. White.[135]

After the mass, the large Lopez funeral procession left the church and proceeded west on West Howard Avenue to Cuevas Street. There, it turned south to Beach Road and then west again to the Biloxi Cemetery. The order of the Lopez funeral procession was as follows: Biloxi public school children; members of the Oystermen's Protective Association; Commercial Club members; Ladies of the Sacred Heart Society, United Daughters of the Confederacy and King's Daughters; carriages carrying floral offerings; the carriage of Father Kettels and his assistants; the hearse accompanied by the pallbearers, honorary pallbearers and twelve young ladies dressed in white from the West End School; and, finally, the carriages of the Lopez family followed by many carriages transporting friends and acquaintances of Lazaro Lopez to his final resting place in the Biloxi cemetery.[136]

ARCHBISHOP EUGENE ANTONIO MARINO: THE FIRST BLACK ARCHBISHOP IN THE UNITED STATES

Archbishop Eugene Antonio Marino had the distinction of being the first Black archbishop in the United States, the first Black auxiliary bishop for Washington, D.C., and the first Black secretary of the National Conference of Catholic Bishops.[137]

Marino was born on May 29, 1934, in Biloxi, Mississippi. His father, Jesus Maria Marino, was born in Puerto Rico, and his mother, Lottie Irene Bradford, was from Biloxi. His father worked as a baker, and his mother worked as a maid. He attended Catholic schools in Biloxi and earned his bachelor's degree from St. Joseph Seminary College in Washington, D.C. He went on to study at Loyola University and finally earned a master's degree in religious education from Fordham University. In 1962, he was ordained as a priest of the St. Joseph Society of the Sacred Heart (the Josephites) at the National Shrine of the Immaculate Conception in Washington, D.C. The Josephites is the largest Catholic order whose exclusive mission is to serve the Black community. It was founded in 1871 after the Civil War to mainly minister to the newly freed enslaved people.[138]

Eugene Marino. *Photograph by Chris Cahill.*

After his ordination, he taught religion, biology and physical science for six years at Epiphany College in Newburgh, New York. He served as spiritual director of St. Joseph Seminary for four years before being elected vicar general of the Josephites in 1971.[139]

In 1974, when he was only forty, he became an auxiliary bishop in Washington, D.C., making him only the third Black person to become a bishop of the Catholic Church in the United States. In 1987, he organized a trip for a number of Black Catholics to see Pope John Paul II, and during a talk with these men and women, he stated:

> *Growing up as a young boy in Mississippi, with the double—I was going to say handicap, but I'll say blessing—of being Black and Catholic. I never thought I would see the day when I would be standing here preaching God's holy word in this place as a priest, indeed, as a bishop. Generations of Black Catholics never lived to see a Black priest or sister, let alone ever dream that their son or daughter might become one.*[140]

On May 5, 1988, Marino was installed as the archbishop of Atlanta, becoming the first Black archbishop in U.S. history. While at the Cathedral of Christ the King in Atlanta, he became involved with the growing problem of sexual misconduct of Catholic priests. This was ironic, as the archbishop himself became involved in a sexual relationship with a female member of the parish.[141]

In July 1990, Archbishop Marino suddenly resigned his position in Atlanta, citing personal problems and saying that he wanted to take time off for spiritual renewal and psychological therapy. About a month later, an Atlanta television station broke the story that the archbishop was having a relationship with a young lay minister named Vicki R. Long. Long was a twenty-seven-year-old single mother who revealed that she and Marino had been together for about two years. Long told the television reporter that she and the archbishop had been secretly married since 1988. She revealed that the archbishop had performed a secret wedding ceremony that married the two of them, including the exchange of wedding rings. The archbishop had no choice but to admit to the affair. Archbishop Marino had met Long when she sought counseling for a previous relationship that she had with a priest in Savannah with whom she had a son.[142]

The relationship between the archbishop and Long ended when or shortly before the scandal broke. Soon after publicly expressing his utmost regret over violating his sacred vow of chastity, he quietly left the public eye, accepting a position as a chaplain at the Sisters of Mercy in Alma, Michigan, while retaining his title of archbishop. He underwent a six-week-long period of counseling. Black Catholic leaders throughout the country rallied to his side, mounting a campaign that resulted in twenty-five thousand letters of support titled "To Archbishop Marino with Love."

On November 12, 2000, while acting as a counselor for the personal problems of fellow priests and nuns at Salesian High School in New Rochelle, New York, Archbishop Eugene Marino died of an apparent heart attack at the St. Ignatius Retreat House, Manhasset, New York, where he was living. He was discovered in his bed by the housekeeper.[143]

A mass of resurrection was held by the Salesians on Wednesday, November 15, 2000, in New Rochelle. The Josephites also offered a mass on Thursday, November 16, at St. Francis Xavier Church in Baltimore. His body was sent back to his hometown of Biloxi, where a wake was held on Sunday, November 19, at Our Mother of Sorrows Church at 815 Division Street, Biloxi. Visitation was held on Monday, November 20, from 10:00 to 11:00 a.m., at the Cathedral of the Nativity of the Blessed Virgin Mary in Biloxi. A mass of resurrection was also offered at the cathedral on Monday at 11:00 a.m.[144]

Archbishop Eugene Marino was buried in the Old Biloxi Cemetery.

George Edgar Ohr: Considered to be the First "Art" Potter in the United States and a Forerunner of the American Abstract-Expressionism Movement

George Edgar Ohr was born on July 12, 1857. He is considered by many to be the first "art" potter in the United States and by some to be a forerunner of the American Abstract-Expressionism movement for his innovative creations in clay pottery.[145] Characteristically, that style of art tends to be abstract, innovative and futuristic. American Abstract-Expressionism marked the beginning of American art as a distinct form that broke with the traditional European traditions that shaped artistic conventions until that time. The movement benefited from the African, Caribbean, Asian and European folk cultures that had immigrated to the United States. Ohr's innovative pottery was characterized by its thin walls, metallic glazes and twisted and pinched shapes. Ohr created these distinctive pieces using a pottery wheel, something that only a few potters have been able to imitate.[146]

George Edgar Ohr. *Photograph by Chris Cahill.*

George Ohr's parents, George Ohr Sr. and Johanna Wiedman, were German immigrants who first arrived in New Orleans in 1853 from Alsatia, the region in Eastern France on the west bank of the upper Rhine River, next to Switzerland and Germany. The couple met and married in New Orleans, and after a brief stay, they moved to Biloxi, where George Sr. opened the first blacksmith shop in the city, while Ohr's mother, Johanna, operated a popular grocery store, one of the first food markets in Biloxi.[147]

George was a typical teenager, not quite sure what his future would be. His father taught him the blacksmithing business, but the boy was not satisfied. When he was fourteen, he moved to New Orleans, where he tried working numerous jobs. His fate changed when a childhood friend from Biloxi, Joseph Fortuné Meyer, offered him a job as a potter's apprentice. Meyer's family was from the same area of Alsatia as George's parents. This opportunity set the course of George Ohr's life. Ohr later wrote, "When I found the potter's wheel, I felt it all over, like a wild duck in water."

After learning the techniques of pottery making, he left Meyer and went on a two-year, sixteen-state excursion, visiting various potteries throughout the country as a way to further polish his craft. In 1884, Ohr exhibited his work at the World's Industrial and Cotton Centennial Exposition in New Orleans.[148]

While at the World's Fair, he met Josephine Gehring (September 25, 1868–March 17, 1930). He moved back to Biloxi in 1885, and on September 15,

1886, George and Josephine were married. The couple would go on to have ten children, but only five survived to adulthood.[149]

Soon after his return to Biloxi, Meyer contacted Ohr again and offered him a position working with him at his newly formed New Orleans Art Pottery Shop. Ohr worked there from 1888 to 1898, until Meyer's shop closed. He returned again to Biloxi, where he opened his own shop with a renewed determination to succeed. Ohr built his shop, which he called Biloxi Art and Novelty Pottery, completely on his own. He was able to construct his own pottery wheel, a kiln and other necessary tools. He also constructed his building out of lumber he floated down the river.

Ohr cultivated a persona as the "Mad Potter of Biloxi."[150] He grew a wild mustache and posted some eccentric photographs of himself to promote his work. He had a natural flair for showmanship, and this image was perfectly suited for his wild pottery designs. His pottery shop became a popular tourist attraction. Unfortunately, like other visionaries, his talent was not appreciated during his lifetime, and he sold virtually none of his work. Always confident in himself and his designs, he predicted, "I am making pottery for art's sake, God's sake, the future generation, and—by present indications—for my own satisfaction, but when I'm gone, my work...will be prized, honored and cherished."[151]

In 1894, the great Biloxi fire completely destroyed Ohr's workshop, along with much of the downtown area. Ohr referred to the few pieces he was able to save as his charred "clay babies." It wasn't long before George had rebuilt a new pottery shop, which he called Biloxi Art Pottery Unlimited, and his business returned to normal, with tourists flocking to see this eccentric character and his quirky pottery designs.

Meyer, who had taken a position as potter at Sophie Newcomb College, later a part of Tulane University, asked Ohr to join him again in New Orleans. Ohr agreed, since he needed the extra income to support his large family. So, from 1897 to 1899, George traveled back and forth from Biloxi to New Orleans, working two jobs.

In 1904, he won a silver medal at the Louisiana Purchase International Exposition for the most original art pottery. Unfortunately, his prices were too high, and he sold nothing. Although he sought success and recognition for his work, he refused to lower his prices to a point that would allow him to achieve his life's goal.

In 1909, he gave up on being a potter and closed his pottery shop for good. He was urged by his family to sell the remaining works at whatever price he could get, just to clear them out, but instead, he carefully packed up each piece and stored them away in the back of his building, a building that his sons had turned into an auto body repair shop. He was convinced that, one day, the world would recognize him as "the greatest art potter on earth."

On April 7, 1918, Biloxi's mad potter succumbed to throat cancer. George Edgar Ohr died relatively unknown.[152]

In 1968, fifty years after his death, George Ohr's work was finally discovered when an antique dealer from New Jersey, James W. Carpenter, came to the Ohr Brothers Auto Repair Shop, looking for old automobiles, and came across George's "clay babies," which had been lovingly packed away at the back of the shop half a century before. Carpenter realized the value in these treasures and purchased the entire group of about six thousand for a grand price of $50,000. Once his pottery began to hit the market, collectors and art historians began to recognize the value of these distinctive works. Not only did Ohr's work finally begin to sell, but they were selling for thousands of dollars each.

In 1994, the people of Biloxi, who once considered George Ohr only a quirky eccentric, took note of his growing fame by establishing the George E. Ohr Arts and Cultural Center to display his work. In 2003, the "Mad Potter of Biloxi" achieved his ultimate success when the Ohr-O'Keefe Museum of Art opened, designed by the world-famous architect Frank Gehry.

George and his wife, Josephine, were buried in the Old Biloxi Cemetery.

ANTHONY V. RAGUSIN: CREDITED WITH BRINGING KEESLER AIR FORCE BASE TO BILOXI

Anthony V. Ragusin, born on April 22, 1902, was affectionately known as "Mr. Biloxi" and is generally credited with bringing Keesler Air Force Base to the city. For over forty years, he headed the Biloxi Chamber of Commerce. Mayor A.J. Holloway said of Ragusin, "He lived and breathed Biloxi. Thousands of people found out about the beauty of our area and our hospitality through Mr. Tony's published stories and photographs."[153]

In the late nineteenth and early twentieth centuries, the Gulf Coast economy exploded, thanks to the bountiful amounts of seafood and timber. Tourism was also on the rise, with northerners discovering the great climate of South Mississippi. Fabulous hotels like the Great Southern in Gulfport and the Buena Vista in Biloxi offered a luxury vacation at a reasonable price, but the large seafood hauls began to taper off and the great forests that at

Anthony Ragusin. *Photograph by Chris Cahill.*

one time seemed endless were almost all logged out. Tourism remained the most viable source of revenue, but with the devastating impact of the Great Depression of the mid-1930s, the city officials knew that tourism alone could not sustain the city.

Anthony V. Ragusin, the commerce secretary at the time, along with Biloxi mayor Louis Braun and other city officials, began searching for additional ways to attract visitors to the coast. The obvious need was for a commercial airport to improve access to the city. The Civil Aeronautics Administration approved a plan to build a commercial airport northwest of the city's business district. The initial proposal included a large hangar, weather station, beacon light and a three-thousand-foot-long runway. Funding was provided by the Works Projects Administration (WPA), and by 1935, work had begun on Biloxi's new airport.

In 1938, the army air corps conducted military maneuvers at the airport, which was, at that time, the largest peacetime military operation in the South since the Civil War. In the summer of 1938, President Franklin D. Roosevelt (January 30, 1882–April 12, 1945) warned America of a growing danger to world peace, as certain totalitarian regimes were coming to power in Europe and the Far East. The nation's defenses had long been neglected, and Roosevelt sensed a need to modernize the military. He proposed a great increase in government spending. There was tremendous opposition to a military buildup, but in the end, Congress finally agreed to allow for the president's military expansion. This program included enlarging the air corps. The plan included increasing the air force to almost ten times to a level of ten thousand modern combat-ready planes. Increasing the number of planes would also mean that huge numbers of additional airmen would be needed, along with other support personnel, such as aircraft and engine mechanics. Existing training facilities were inadequate to handle the large number of trainees needed.

In April 1939, city officials saw a possible opportunity and asked members of Congress from Mississippi to get them more information about the new pilots' training program. After waiting for almost a year without any response, Biloxi finally received disappointing news. The War Department did not want to build facilities in coastal towns because of their perceived vulnerability to enemy naval attacks.

Once war had broken out in Europe, the army air corps' training facilities were quickly filled to capacity. As a result, the War Department intended to build two new training bases. In the hopes that a training facility would be less of a risk for attack, Chamber of Commerce Secretary Ragusin prepared a proposal for Brigadier General Rush B. Lincoln, the official who would make the decision for the two sites. Ragusin made a strong plea and included the use of the new Biloxi airport to improve the city's chances. He even offered access improvements and additional land for school facilities. This was good enough for the general, who sent two of his staff members down to review the area. They were impressed with the location, the climate and the strong community support.

The army's interest prompted the city to take quick action. Biloxi completed paving the runway and included additional land to support a 5,200-man technical training school. Biloxi, along with one other site, had been chosen for final consideration. In the meantime, the war had expanded and the need for training increased for as many as 24,000 troops. The city immediately added the Biloxi Golf Club's course and clubhouse, the Wilkes Boy Scout Camp, a softball park and several privately owned pieces of land to the proposal. This was the just what the army needed, and on March 6, 1941, Mayor Braun was officially notified that Biloxi had been selected as the site of the new training facility. The construction of the base, which was the most expensive government project ever undertaken in Mississippi, was just the shot in the arm that the coast economy needed.

The base opened on June 12, 1941. The base had not yet been named, and the city officials hoped to have it named after a notable local figure, but it was the War Department's policy to name bases after service members who had been killed in action. They informed Biloxi officials that it would be named in honor of Second Lieutenant Samuel Reeves Keesler Jr. of Greenwood, Mississippi.[154]

Anthony V. Ragusin died on March 3, 1997, at the age of ninety-four. He was buried in the Old Biloxi Cemetery.[155]

PLEASANT REED: ONE OF THE FIRST FREED PEOPLE TO BUILD AND OWN A HOUSE IN BILOXI

Pleasant Reed was born into slavery. The house he built for his family has become known as the Pleasant Reed House. It is one of the first documented houses that was built and owned outright by a freed enslaved person in Biloxi.[156]

Reed was born in 1854 on a plantation in Perry County in the vicinity of Hattiesburg, Mississippi. He and his parents, Benjamin and Charlotte Reed, were enslaved by plantation owner John B. Reed. In 1869, Pleasant Reed moved to Biloxi, along with other members of his family who had drifted to the coast after their emancipation. After moving to Biloxi, Reed worked as a carpenter. While living on the coast, Pleasant met Georgia Anna Harris from Louisiana. She could read and write, and as a native of the pelican state, she could speak both English and Cajun French. Pleasant and Georgia were married on January 23, 1884. The couple eventually had five children: Manuel, Victoria, Percy, Theresa and Paul. In addition to being a carpenter, Pleasant Reed supported the family by making fishnets and selling them to the fishermen along the coast.[157]

With hard work and determination, Reed purchased some land in May 1887 from Jacob Elmer. The property on Elmer Street in Biloxi would become the location of the historic Pleasant Reed house. The house was constructed in a common style for the region that ensured some cross-ventilation for the hot coastal weather. Known as an altered side-hall, camelback Creole cottage, it was built with only three rooms running off of a side hall. The floor plan provided privacy for such a small space. The kitchen that was originally in the backyard was not attached to the house, but the two were eventually joined around 1910, when the house was connected to the public water supply.

Being a carpenter by trade, Pleasant Reed added some charming touches to the small house. Although he was not a master carpenter, he had the desire and ability to add features that set his simple little house apart. He

Pleasant Reed. *Photograph by Chris Cahill.*

used vertical beadboard on the walls, which were whitewashed to give a clean, spacious look to the interior. He added a long room over the kitchen that the Cajuns called a garconnière, meaning "a boy's room." It served as a dormitory-type bedroom for the Reed boys. Pleasant added such small details as a spindle frieze across the front porch, which gave the house the appearance of being something much more than a simple worker's cottage. By 1908, the Reed family was one of the more prominent and successful Black families in Biloxi.[158]

Pleasant Reed died in 1936 at the age of eighty-two. His wife, Georgia, had died three years earlier. Their daughter Therese inherited the house, living there until the 1970s. When she left the house, it was in poor condition and needed many repairs. In 1978, the house was purchased by the Mississippi Gulf Coast Alumnae Chapter of the Delta Sigma Theta sorority. Through their efforts, the iconic house was on its way to being restored. In 2000, the sorority donated the house to the Ohr-O'Keefe Museum of Art in Biloxi, recognizing the importance of the house to the history of the coast. The museum moved the house from its original location on Elmer Street to the grounds of the museum on Highway 90. The house was opened to the public as a museum in May 2003, having been completely restored to its original 1910 appearance.[159]

On August 29, 2005, Hurricane Katrina struck the coast, destroying many of the old historic buildings between Bay St. Louis and Pascagoula. The Pleasant Reed House was one of the buildings that was destroyed. Unfortunately, much of the antique furniture and decorative items were also lost. Because of the historical significance of the house, an extensive collection of archival material had been safely stored. With this available material, it was possible for the museum to construct a perfect replica of the house. Called the Pleasant Reed Interpretive Center, the Ohr-O'Keefe Museum of Art opened the house to the public on September 29, 2008. The house is used to educate the public about the Reed legacy and the importance of Black culture to the Biloxi Area.[160]

WALTER A. WHITE AND CORA WHITE: OWNERS AND FOUNDERS OF THE ICONIC WHITE HOUSE HOTEL

Judge Walter A. White was a respected judge and member of the Mississippi State legislature, but he, along with his wife, Cora, were best known as the owners and founders of the iconic White House Hotel.

Walter White was born in Rankin County, near Jackson, on December 1, 1884. He studied law under Governor A.J. McLaurin. After passing the bar, he practiced law in Brandon, Mississippi, for seven years. In 1887, he married his first wife, Harriet "Hattie" Enochs (July 21, 1861–September 24, 1889), with whom he had four daughters: Cora, Lula, Laura and Nell.[161] Hattie died prematurely at the age of twenty-eight and was buried in her hometown of Crystal Springs, Mississippi. A few years after her death, Walter married Hattie's younger sister Cora. Cora was born on June 27, 1864. The two sisters grew up on the plantation of their parents, Captain I.V. Enochs and Julia Harriet Enochs, outside of Jackson. Cora attended Whitworth College, an all-female school located in Brookhaven, Mississippi, where she graduated in 1885. She married Walter White in 1890, and the Whites moved to Biloxi. That same year, their first child, Harry, was born, but he died as an infant. They later had two other sons, Walter Enochs and Johnnie Theodore.[162]

When they arrived on the coast, the Whites lived in Pass Christian at the Mexican Gulf Hotel, later known as the Palmer House. The Mexican Gulf was the first hotel on the Gulf Coast that was specifically designed to attract winter guests from northern states. It was comfortable living for the Whites.

Walter and Cora White. *Photograph by Chris Cahill.*

In 1885, Charles Dyer wrote in his book *Along the Gulf*, "The Mexican Gulf Hotel is, by long odds, the finest hotel architecturally on the entire coast, and its interior decorations and furnishings are beautiful in the extreme, so much so in fact as to cause the management of this house to be greatly envied by many of the other hotel keepers of the coast."[163]

After the initial period of hotel living, Walter bought a home for the family on Magnolia Avenue in Biloxi, where they lived for about a year. In 1893, he sold their home on Magnolia Avenue and purchased the land at 1550 West Beach Boulevard in Biloxi. This was the original site of the Gorenflo Oyster Company, which had just been destroyed by a strong hurricane that devastated the coast that year. White was able to salvage thousands of oyster shells, which he used to fill in low marshy areas that were present on the huge piece of property. This created high ground on which to build his new Victorian mansion. The judge planted seven live oaks on the sloping lawn to complement the beautiful panoramic view of the gulf.[164]

In Biloxi, Walter practiced law under Judge J.H. Neville. After a number of years working with Judge Neville, he was elected to the Mississippi State legislature, where he served for one term. In 1896, he left the legislature after being appointed district attorney. In 1904, he gave up his job as district attorney to go into private law practice with I.J. Ford of Pascagoula. He and Ford continued as partners until Ford's death in 1915. In 1925, he was appointed circuit judge to fill an unexpired term. After that partial term was up, he ran for that position and won, serving as circuit judge for several more terms until his retirement in 1939 due to his poor health.[165]

In 1899, while Walter was busy establishing his early law practice, his wife, Cora, began taking in boarders to help the young family financially. First, there was a business associate of Judge White, and soon, there were other boarders, mostly local schoolteachers. As Walter's law practice grew, so did the demand for rooms to accommodate the influx of visitors from the North who were just discovering the area's warm climate and beautiful beaches. With an inadequate number of hotel rooms in the area, Cora saw a golden opportunity. She made the decision to operate a boardinghouse to accommodate the need. The enterprising Cora printed a sheet listing the cost of a room at her house as well as the cost of room and board for those who so requested. She sent the list to all of the guests who had already stayed at the house, reminding people that it would be prudent to make reservations before their arrival to ensure that a room would be available. By 1904, Cora had developed a solid client base of summer guests.[166]

Walter's law practice was growing, leaving him little time to help Cora look after the guests. It wasn't long before Cora realized she was getting tired of the boardinghouse arrangement. Cooking, cleaning and providing entertainment for the guests was getting old. The business was growing so fast that she and Walter decided to expand even further. In 1911, Walter purchased the adjacent Burke house. The two buildings were connected, and a lobby was created to give the appearance of a unified establishment. Cora also added a large front porch with classical columns and a second-story balcony, a dining room and a ballroom for dancing.

This new addition was still not adequate for her growing business, so the Whites ultimately bought five more adjacent houses. Architect George B. Rogers, who had designed the Bellingrath mansion in Mobile, was brought over to tie the seven Victorian houses together in a viable unit. Rogers's work converted the seven residences into the magnificent White House Hotel. By 1910, at least one travel publication had designated Cora's creation as "the leading hotel of Biloxi."[167]

Walter and Cora's sons, Walter and John, joined their mother in growing the hotel business. On September 7, 1934, Cora died. After her death, the family decided to sell the hotel, and the White House was purchased by Jimmie Love Jr. Love, the owner of WLOX Radio and, later, WLOX Television, was also the owner of the Buena Vista Hotel. He was very successful in promoting both hotels until Hurricane Camille severely damaged the buildings. Love sold the two hotels in 1971.

Judge Walter A. White died on April 8, 1942, at the age of eighty-seven. Both he and Cora were buried in the Old Biloxi Cemetery.

THE YOUNGHANS FAMILY (PERRY YOUNGHANS, MARIA YOUNGHANS AND MIRANDA YOUNGHANS): BILOXI LIGHTHOUSE KEEPERS FOR OVER SIXTY YEARS

Maria Younghans; her husband, Perry; and their daughter, Miranda, are known in coast history as the family who faithfully kept the Biloxi Lighthouse operating for over sixty years.

President George Washington had placed all lighthouses in the United States under the supervision of the secretary of the treasury. The fifth auditor of the treasury, Stephen Pleasonton (1777–1855), became the man in charge.[168] In 1847, Pleasonton announced that he intended to place a cast-iron lighthouse in Biloxi. Following a $12,000 appropriation by Congress on March 3, 1847, the Biloxi Lighthouse was constructed. It became the first cast-iron tower in the South. The importance of an iron tower was proven in 1998, when Hurricane Georges destroyed the masonry tower at Round Island. This left the Biloxi Lighthouse as the last standing of the more than ten lighthouses that were originally built along the Gulf Coast. John Fayard sold one acre of land to the government for $600; there, it built the tower. The metal plates that were used in its construction were cast in Baltimore by the Murray and Hazlehurst Vulcan Works for $6,347. The tower was completed in the spring of 1848, with Marcellus J. Howard as the first lighthouse keeper.[169] Howard served until 1854, when he was replaced by Mary J. Reynolds. In 1866, Perry Younghans, the third lighthouse keeper, became the first of the Younghans family to serve in that capacity. Sadly, Perry died in 1867, after only one year on the job. Perry's wife, Maria, continued with his duties and was selected to officially take his place.

Maria Younghans was born in Biloxi on January 20, 1842, and was only twenty-five years old when she became the new lighthouse keeper. Nothing would stop Maria from carrying out her duties, regardless of how difficult the situation. She kept the light burning even when it seemed impossible to do so. In 1893, a hurricane struck, heavily damaging the base of the tower. An article in the *New Orleans Daily Picayune* on October 21, 1893, commented on Maria's dedication to her actions during the storm, "At Biloxi, Mrs.

Younghans family. *Photograph by Chris Cahill.*

Younghans, the plucky woman who was in charge of the light, kept a light going all through the storm, notwithstanding the fact that there were several feet of water in the room where she lived."

As Maria got older, her daughter Miranda would help her mother operate the lighthouse. Finally, on December 31, 1918, at the age of seventy-seven, when Maria retired, Miranda was immediately selected to take her mother's position as keeper. Miranda, who was born on April 24, 1857, was not young. She was sixty-one years old when she became the new lighthouse keeper. Maria passed away on August 20, 1925, leading the Lighthouse Service to comment on her long tenure: "Maria had a perfectly clear record and the highest approval for her services."

Miranda Younghans remained at her post until she retired on April 23, 1929, ending the exemplary service of the Younghans family to Biloxi. Miranda died on February 5, 1933, at the age of seventy-five. All of the Younghans family members were buried in the Old Biloxi Cemetery.

The light of the Biloxi Lighthouse was automated in 1940, bringing an end to the job of lighthouse keeper. Mr. Joseph J. Oliver was the last person to hold that position.

ST. CYR (JOSEPH SEYMOUR) ZAMOR: THE PATRIARCH OF THE SEYMOUR FAMILY ON THE GULF COAST

The entire Seymour family of the Mississippi Gulf Coast can trace their roots to St. Cyr (Joseph Seymour) Zamor. As with other old family names from that period, the origin of the name is confusing. The name on Zamor's tombstone is St. Cyr Zamor, yet the name appears in various Catholic church documents as St. Cyr LeBlanc, St. Cyr White, José St. Cyr, St. Cyr Zamora, José Zamora and Joseph S. Moore. In a July 1995 article written by Brother Jerome Lepre in the *Mississippi Coast History and Genealogical Society Journal*, the progression of the name is given as LeBlanc-White-Moore-Zamora-Seymour. The name Seymour has survived in various forms, such as Seamore, Seymore, Seymoure and, finally, Seymour. The name probably derived as a result of someone writing the name the way it sounded to the uneducated ear. It is not a stretch to see how the name Zamor would sound like Seymour to someone who spoke a different language.

St. Cyr Zamor was born in 1781 in Pascagoula, Mississippi. His father was Charles LeBlanc from New Orleans, and his mother was Genevieve Catherine Baudreau. The couple was married on September 1, 1783. Genevieve was the daughter of Jean Baptiste Baudreau dit Graveline and Marie Louise (Fayard) Baudreau. The word *dit* in the old records meant "known as" or "called." Graveline became one of the wealthiest men in the colony.

Jean Baptiste Baudreau was born on May 18, 1671, in Montreal, Quebec, Canada, and was one of the first settlers to travel with Pierre le Moyne d'Iberville to colonize the Gulf Coast. Graveline arrived in 1700 on the ship *La Renomme*. In 1702, he and the other French pioneers moved to Fort Saint Louis, north of the city of Mobile. Graveline was a great supporter of the young colony, making frequent trips to France to bring people to the area. He also traveled to Vera Cruz and Havana, where he was the first to import purebred cattle. He made his fortune by trading furs, cattle and agricultural goods.[170]

In June 1808, St. Cyr Zamor married Marie-Josephe Ryan, the daughter of Jean Ryan and Marie Gargaret in New Orleans. St. Cyr worked as a sailor and a fisherman, in addition to raising cattle and farming. He settled in what is now Jackson County, in the area that has become known as Fontainebleau (Belle Fountain). The couple had eight children: Edward, Pierre, Jean-Baptiste, Lazarus, Narcisse, Victoria, Josephine and St. Cyr II.[171]

On January 1, 1845, St. Cyr was aboard a boat in the gulf when the ship encountered a heavy storm. Several barrels were lined up on the deck, and during the tossing of the waves, one broke loose and accidentally struck St.

St. Cyr Zamor. *Photograph by Chris Cahill.*

Cyr, causing internal injuries. He was dead by the time the ship returned to port in New Orleans. He was only fifty-seven.[172]

After his death, his children continued to live on the land, selling off various pieces until 1914. In April 1944, Reverend Herbert Mullin and Monsignor Geofrey O'Connell, Roman Catholic Irish priests, acquired the property from Charles S. Gerth of New Orleans.[173] The two priests, along with the Brothers of the Sacred Heart from Bay St. Louis, created a camp for young boys and girls, which they called Camp Graveline. The camp offered fishing, swimming, sailing, waterskiing, hiking and horseback riding. The camp was later acquired by the Sisters of Mercy, who operated it from May 1958 to March 1961, when it was purchased by Father Mullin and others.[174] The camp continued to operate until the late 1950s. The camp site was destroyed by Hurricane Camille in August 1969.

St. Cyr Zamor, the first of the Seymour family on the Gulf Coast, was buried in a vault in the Old Biloxi Cemetery. It was discovered during a restoration of the tomb in 2019 that his wife, Marie-Josephe, was also buried with him in the tomb.

4
THE TOMB BOOM

By Nick Black

When the Biloxi Cemetery began to receive its first burials, it was the epitome of a picturesque coastal graveyard; majestic live oaks, sandy soil, gulf breezes all helping form an ideal atmosphere for the deceased to settle. Although the perfect landscape makes this particular cemetery memorable, its formation, design and function are those of most local cemeteries along the Gulf Coast, especially for the period in which it opened. Picturing the old graveyard with only headstones sitting among the trees is now difficult. At first glance, when driving down Beach Boulevard, tombs are now the most recognizable features that distinguish the site as a cemetery. These structures, however, are far from being new.

The transition between in-ground burials to tombs occurred over time. Comparisons between the Old Biloxi Cemetery and the cemeteries of New Orleans have become difficult over the past two hundred years. However, this was not always the case. Cemeteries such as Lafayette No. 1 (New Orleans's oldest municipal cemetery), which dates back to the 1830s, was once a place with many in-ground burials scattered among tombs. The same may be said of the city's largest (in interments) cemetery, Greenwood (founded in 1852). Although these grounds were developed decades after the Biloxi Cemetery's first burials, they both had periods of time when tomb development was at its peak. Like many New Orleans cemeteries, Greenwood saw this occur between the 1850s and 1870s. During this time, a new era of tomb development rose on a scale that had not yet been seen before. One hundred miles away, Biloxi witnessed a similar evolution in its cemetery.

It goes without saying that the cultural ties between New Orleans and the Mississippi Gulf Coast are in unison with each other. Biloxi was and remains a getaway for many New Orleanians. It should be of no surprise that trends between the two cities occurred simultaneously. Although Biloxi has always been a much smaller city, both geographically and in population, the two cities shared blood. During the mid-nineteenth century, there was hardly a family along the Gulf Coast that did not have some tie to New Orleans. Generally speaking, cemeteries were not exempt from this.

Similar to the beginnings of many municipal cemeteries, the land for the Biloxi Cemetery was deeded to the city. By the time this occurred in 1844, the site had been developed and was already being used as a graveyard. Although we may only speculate as to when the first person was laid to rest there, we know concretely that 1829, monuments were being erected. By the time of the earliest known burial, the cemetery would have resembled a churchyard. Like many early-nineteenth-century churchyards, there were no established aisles or paving, nor were plots being numbered or mapped. General order was likely not well defined in the Biloxi Cemetery. Once a cemetery begins in such a way, it will remain that way unless markers are moved, the ground turned and the cemetery reestablished, with burials taking place over previous ones. This process would not have occurred overnight; instead, it is often slow and drawn out. Regardless, this is typically only done when there is a lack of usable space or in instances of a demand for prime locations (for example, a waterfront view). Some New Orleans cemeteries throughout the past two centuries have been completely buried over. Although it is unlikely that this was done so on a similar scale in Biloxi, it is quite possible that the cemetery grounds we see today have more individuals buried in them than we will possibly ever know.

Biloxi was a close-knit community, a city where residents knew each other, and certain surnames were prominent. Many families were interconnected through marriages, which helped create stronger community ties. Individual plots in the cemetery where families buried their dead gives us a glimpse as to when the landscape of the city began to change. The transition of some families to using tombs instead of the ground for burials began as early as the late 1820s and early 1830s. With this being said, we are limited to knowing the history of the structures that are no longer present in the cemetery. Our knowledge is based on what tombs still exist today. Additionally, old photographs and written history contribute to this. Unfortunately, the exact age of many tombs is questionable when there is no tablet or door present.

However, regardless of these challenges, certain key details in each tomb's construction sheds light on its history.

One of the earliest tombs built—if not the first—in Biloxi was for Marguerite Babin (who died in 1829). Unfortunately, all that is left of the tomb is the marble tablet that once covered the opening of its vault. The bottom-right corner of the tablet bears the signature "F. & J. Kain, New Orleans." Kain was a stonecutter in New Orleans, where the tablet of Babin was furnished. Around this time (late 1820s–early 1830s), the monument business in New Orleans was progressing. Stonecutters from different ethnicities arrived in the Crescent City as the industry began to erupt.

Throughout the nineteenth century, many monument men acted as cemetery sextons (operators of the graveyard), tomb builders and stonecutters. In some instances, these men extended their businesses to undertaking as well. During the first half of the century, the Mississippi Coast was far too rural to have stonecutters of its own. It is likely that agents for New Orleans monument dealers were available on request to fill the demand for local cemetery work. Similar to most industries, stone-cutting had its first competitive market in the Northeast. From cities such as New York, Boston and Philadelphia rose monument companies that would have agents in many major cities. Francis and James Kain, for example, was a New York firm that presumably arrived in New Orleans during the 1820s. The business sold an assortment of marble for buildings in addition to chimney pieces, monuments, tombs and gravestones.[175] Whereas many tombs in New Orleans were being built by stonecutters and builders who specialized in the trade, Biloxi's first tombs were not.

From the 1820s to late 1840s, the tombs constructed in the cemetery were single-vault rectangular boxes with roofs usually comprising two tiers of descending size. The "platform tombs," as they are called, were of the most basic form in both style and function. In comparison to the tombs that were being built in New Orleans at the same time, there was an absence of elaborate sepulchers in Biloxi. The platform tombs were quite modest, and it is likely that their simple construction and lack of ornate detailing was directly influenced by the ease with which one could be built. To construct one of these tombs, a foundation of bricks was laid on the ground, where four walls were erected. The roof structure was then formed by using a stepped design, also made from brick. Once the structure was erected, the brick was covered with lime-based stucco. Following an interment, the vault opening was sealed with bricks, and an engraved tablet bearing the name and death date of the deceased was placed over it.

Right: Marble tablet from the tomb of Marguerite Babin (1829), believed to be the oldest marked grave in the cemetery. *Photograph by Nick Black.*

Below: An example of a single-vault platform tomb, the most basic form of tomb construction. *Photograph by Chris Cahill.*

From the 1830s to the 1860s, tombs in Biloxi changed very little in style or construction. Nevertheless, there are key details that differentiate those built before the middle of the nineteenth century and those constructed after. From the exterior, these monuments have little contrast; however, this changes when viewed from the inside. The most significant change that occurred was in how the structures' roofs were built. Barrel vaults came to replace the older stepped brick design. Whereas the former method of stacking bricks was the simplest way of enclosing the top of a tomb (when using only bricks), barrel vaults were a bit more sophisticated. Skill became necessary for creating vaulted roofs. When properly built, a vaulted roof is far more superior in strength than a stepped one. Over the past 170 years, this had proven to be a critical aspect in how a tomb withstands neglect and deterioration.

The first visible change regarding tombs occurred in the late 1840s to early 1850s with the development of multi-vault tombs. Although monuments that allowed for more than one or two interments was not a new concept, it was just being seen for the first time in Biloxi. The platform design remained in use; however, the structures' heights were adjusted to allow for two-barrel vaults. The lower barrel vault divided the tomb in

Above: A subterranean chamber called a "caveau." *Photograph by John Cuevas.*

Opposite: A view of the opened Juan de Cuevas vault during its restoration. *Photograph by Chris Cahill.*

half while acting as the shelf for the upper crypt. Another feature of these larger monuments was the "receiving vault" or "caveau," a subterranean chamber that housed only remains. Before a new interment could occur, the remnants of the existing casket on either the upper or lower shelf were removed, and the remains of the person were placed into the receiving vault. In order for a casket to be placed in the lower vault without falling into this receptacle, removable boards or pipes were installed perpendicularly to the side walls. In essence, this created a removable shelf that a casket could rest on while also providing access to the receiving vault when necessary.

Whereas a single vault tomb was large enough to allow for only one casket and a couple sets of remains pushed to the back wall, a raised "family tomb" with a receiving vault permitted unlimited burials. The first upright two-vault platform tomb of this design in the Biloxi Cemetery was the one in which Juan de Cuevas was interred.

The materials that were used to construct tombs in the Old Biloxi Cemetery provide insight to the city's local industry and the availability of products during the mid-nineteenth century. In regard to tombs being built, bricks were the only permanent material that would have been available to builders. Local brickmaking has been traced back to the beginnings of Biloxi's settlement. In fact, a brick factory is mentioned in a letter sent by D'Iberville in 1703. Records also account that by the time the capital moved to New Orleans, brick production had become fairly largescale.[176] The necessity of brick was a driving force for individuals to open brickyards and for companies to form. Importing bricks from the Crescent City was quite common during the first half of the nineteenth century, and the Biloxi Cemetery provides proof of this. In 1845, brick from the factory of Evariste Blanc was imported from New Orleans and used to construct the tomb of St. Cyr Zamor (Sancere Seymour).

Biloxi's first notable brickyard that revolutionized the region's brick manufacturing industry did not arrive until the middle of the nineteenth century. William Grey Kendall took advantage of the demand for high-quality bricks. As a result, he constructed a plant on Biloxi's Back Bay. In fact, the land Kendall acquired was that of the Old French colonial brickyard, a site that produced bricks for some of New Orleans's earliest establishments. Kendall's operation of the "Biloxi Steam Brick Works" was one of the first—if not the first—manufacturer in the area to utilize the development of a steam-powered machine to produce bricks. By 1849, William Kendall became renowned for his "Biloxi firebrick." The popularity of this product increased when Kendall was awarded a contract to supply brick for a new Customs House building in New Orleans. In 1850, advertisements began to appear, claiming Kendall's bricks were superior to lake bricks (those produced from clays along Lake Pontchartrain). However, it was the resistance to fire that made his bricks so well known. Tests were created throughout the region by reputable businesses to showcase the quality of the brick. One experiment included the construction of walls made from lake brick, country brick and firebrick. The walls were then burned, followed by cooling with water. This particular test resulted in only the Biloxi firebrick surviving.[177] Due to the bricks' tolerance to heat,

William Grey Kendall revolutionized the region's brick manufacturing industry. *Photograph by Jason Taylor.*

it was often sold to sugar planters or those constructing furnaces. For many years, William H. Eager was Kendall's agent in New Orleans who represented the Biloxi Steam Brick Works. It was reported in the *New Orleans Crescent* that 300,000 bricks were being produced each week. As a result, advertisements across the area exploited the availability of the brick until the mid-1850s. Biloxi firebrick left its mark across the South, and the Biloxi Cemetery was not an exception.

The fifth decade of the nineteenth century brought a new landscape to the Biloxi Cemetery. Although some tombs were present years prior, the "boom" occurred in a short period of time. It is necessary to note that due to a lack of documentation and records, we must base our knowledge on what exists today. Currently, about half of the twenty-seven platform tombs in the oldest section of the cemetery still have closure tablets/markers present. Of these tombs, five are dated back to the 1850s. Furthermore, based on a survey of the bricks that were used to construct some of these tombs, it can be reasonably concluded that seven of the unmarked tombs were built during this same decade.

There is no single explanation as to the spike in tomb construction during that relatively short period of time. Nevertheless, there were a few fundamental causes that contributed to this. During the 1850s, Biloxi was no longer just a secluded rural fishing port. The hospitality industry was growing rapidly, and several hotels were being established. The skilled labor required to construct these hotels and estates was becoming more readily available. The influx of masons working in the area would have created opportunities for those wanting a tomb. Although still regarded as a small coastal town, Biloxi's industries, including brickmaking, were at an all-time high. With this came the availability of materials on a grander scale. For example, sourcing quality brick from New Orleans or elsewhere was no longer a concern for builders. At the same time, importing and exporting resources between major cities increased. This alone allowed for more agent contracting of men dealing in the monument trade.

The cultural influences regarding burial customs were always present in Biloxi. The Spanish, French and, later, Creole practices of using above-ground structures to house the dead had been in use for centuries in Europe. By the 1850s, the opportunity to do so in Biloxi would have been more accessible. It is worth noting that tombs were built on an "at need" basis. This is especially true for the more rural cemeteries. In order for tomb internment to be an option, it was crucial for there to be builders who could build a structure on short notice. By the middle of the nineteenth century, the science of preserving bodies after death had not yet become a mainstream practice. Consequently, the deceased would be buried or interred twenty-four hours after death. If a tomb could not be constructed within a short period of time, the coffin would need to be temporarily buried or housed until the monument was completed. This would have undoubtedly placed a burden on the family. Furthermore, this often resulted in tombs being hastily built. With this being said, monuments and tombs were constructed for those who could afford them. Ornate tombs would not be seen in Biloxi until the end of the nineteenth century; nonetheless, platform tombs built between the 1840s and 1860s were no less a statement of the families or individuals who commissioned them.

In conclusion, the 1850s tomb "boom" in the old Biloxi Cemetery may be attributed to industry, materials and skilled labor, all of which were products of the city's growth during this time. This, in part with a constant stream of societal influences from cities such as New Orleans, created a demand for such monuments.

The importance of these structures then compared to now has not changed. They are both a reflection of the city and the individuals who once called it home. Over a century and a half later, many still provide their intended function: to protect and memorialize the dead. However, as decades have passed, these structures provide more than a final resting place, they have become guides to a city's past

5

SECRETS OF THE CUEVAS TOMB

The fog was as dense as gumbo on that day in the Old Biloxi Cemetery, when an anthropology team from the University of Southern Mississippi, under the direction of Dr. Marie Danforth, began removing the remains from the old Cuevas tomb. The gloomy atmosphere that hung over the proceedings was appropriate for the task at hand. Slowly and with much care, each fragment of bone, cloth and wood was carefully removed and placed on a table for scientific examination. The wooden fragments of the coffin on the top shelf were amazingly intact, along with various items of casket hardware, including a metal plaque that read "At Rest." The remnants of a beautiful rosary were found clutched sweetly in the lady's hands. A St. Christopher medal was also discovered in the ashes. The high quality of the wood attested to the social standing of the deceased.

While carefully separating and arranging the bones, Dr. Danforth announced a startling discovery. The team had found the remains of a young female child placed lovingly on the chest of Juan de Cuevas. The two bodies were found on the bottom shelf of the tomb. This was not unusual. It would be expected to find the first person who had died on the bottom. Since Marie died four years after Juan, on October 10, 1853, everyone assumed that the person on the top shelf was Marie. But who was this child?

The child was easy to identify. Juan and Marie's sixth child, Marie Anastasie, was born in 1803 at their home on Cat Island. She was the only one of the Cuevases' twelve children to have died before reaching adulthood. According to census records, she was not alive in 1810, which means she

The gloomy atmosphere that hung over the proceedings was appropriate for the task at hand. *Photograph by Jason Taylor.*

Nick Black became the first person to look inside the Cuevas tomb in over one hundred years. *Photograph by Jason Taylor.*

Above: The first view inside the Cuevas tomb. *Photograph by Jason Taylor.*

Left: The anthropology team carefully removed the remains of Juan de Cuevas. *Photograph by Jason Taylor.*

Above: A casket handle and other hardware was found in the Cuevas tomb. *Photograph by Jason Taylor.*

Opposite: A delicate rosary was found clutched sweetly in the lady's hands. *Photograph by Chris Cahill.*

would have been between five or seven years old when she died. This age matches that of the young girl in the tomb. Like her father, Anastasie had been buried on the island, near the family home, prior to being moved to the Old Biloxi Cemetery.

As Dr. Danforth and her team continued their meticulous work, they made an even more startling discovery: the female on the top shelf was not Marie. Marie's body was found to also be on the bottom shelf, along with Juan and the baby. This newly discovered female was estimated to be between twenty-five and twenty-seven years of age. Who was this mysterious young woman? Why was she in the Cuevas family tomb? Everyone was baffled.

Researchers began referring to the Cuevas family tree for answers. They were looking for someone in the immediate family who had died during that period. They knew from the records that Juan de Cuevas died on September 24, 1849, and was first buried near his home on Cat Island.[178] It was originally believed that the tomb in the Old Biloxi Cemetery was built shortly after his death, but the bricks that were used to construct the vault were not manufactured until the 1850s. This means that Marie had also been

Bones found in the Cuevas tomb are carefully cleaned and identified. *Photograph by Jason Taylor.*

Dr. Marie Danforth (*right*) and the anthropology team conducted a meticulous examination of the remains in the Cuevas tomb. *Photograph by Jason Taylor.*

Remains of Juan de Cuevas and the others in the tomb are respectively placed in a newly constructed pine casket. *Photograph by Jason Taylor.*

buried on Cat Island, waiting for the tomb in the Old Biloxi Cemetery to be completed. When it was ready, the remains of Juan, Marie and Anastasie were moved to the new Cuevas family vault. But why were all three bodies moved from their graves on the island? After all, Anastasie had been dead for forty years.

The answer was simple: Juan and Marie had previously sold Cat Island to Judah P. Benjamin on March 13, 1837. The contract gave the Cuevas family a life estate. This meant that Juan and Marie would remain in possession of the island as long as they were living. Once they both had passed away, the new owner would legally take over the island, and the Cuevas family did not want to leave anyone behind on their island home that was then owned by strangers. Not only did Dr. Danforth's evidence point to Anastasie being the young child in the tomb, but the placement of her body in the loving embrace of her father made her identity seem certain. But the mystery woman's identity remained unknown. More information was needed to solve the puzzle.

Just as it looked as though the team had reached a dead end, Nick Black discovered the fragments of a small bottle on the top shelf of the tomb near the young woman's remains. This turned out to be a vital piece of evidence

Deron Cuevas (*right*) and Michael Hoda place the new casket containing all of the remains from the Cuevas tomb back into the vault. *Photograph by Jason Taylor.*

that finally led to a breakthrough. Although it was cracked, it appeared to be a hexagonal-shaped (six-sided) medicine bottle, pale aqua in color, measuring approximately 7 inches high and 2⅜ inches in diameter. The words "Pepto-Mangan (Gude)" were embossed in the glass on one side. This was enough information to identify the manufacturer.

By researching the maker's mark on the bottom of the bottle, along with other indicators, like size, quality of glass and print on the bottle, it was discovered to have been produced between the late 1850s and early 1910s. This gave the researchers a timeframe in which to work. The discovery of the bottle was a game changer, but the most important clue was a scrap of paper found inside the bottle. In the book *Fragile Grounds: Louisiana's Endangered Cemeteries*, the authors state that coffin identification tubes, also known as "memory files," were small bottles placed inside coffins that contained scrolls of paper listing the deceased's name, sex and date of birth. These bottles were used to identify remains if tombs were ever reopened.[179] The bottle and paper had been placed inside the Cuevas tomb to identify the young lady. This was particularly important, since it was determined from the Cuevas family records that the woman was not a blood relative of Juan de Cuevas.

The scroll had deteriorated over time, leaving only a tiny fragment of paper. The writing was faded. Only three partial words, "cuev," "27 years" and "native," were still legible. At first, it was thought to be Juan's obituary because of the word "native," as Juan was always described as a "native" of Spain. But the date did not match the death of Juan de Cuevas.

While searching cemetery records in the Biloxi Library, based on the information that had been uncovered, the one person who matched the information was a young twenty-seven-year-old woman named Sarah Westbrook Cuevas. Several other facts matched. Her obituary stated she was a "native" of New Orleans, and she died in 1909, coinciding with the production date of the bottle (late 1850s–early 1910s). The funeral home records also indicate that the metal plaque on the casket read "At Rest," the same as the one found in the Cuevas tomb. All of the elements seemed to fit. Could this be the mystery woman?

6
THE MYSTERY WOMAN

For generations, the Cuevas family believed that only Juan and his wife, Marie, were buried in the Cuevas tomb, but during the restoration, an unidentified woman was also found in the tomb. Who was this mystery woman?

On January 4, 1890, Ella A. Giles, a special correspondent from the *Wisconsin State Journal* wrote about a Captain Charles Joseph Cuevas and a trip she took with him to Cat Island:

> *Twelve miles in the bow of the clean and prettily painted little tug plied by Captain Spotswood between Biloxi and Ship Island every day, brought us in sight of Cat Island, on which the Great Sand Hill is located. The white summit of the dune was visible much farther away. The tug could get no nearer than within three miles of the beach, but there was the schooner being towed in its wake, and the trustworthy old seaman, Capt. (Charles Joseph) Cuevas, to sail it, and when the schooner could get no nearer than within half a mile, there was the skiff being towed in its wake, which Capt. Cuevas rowed as far as it could go, and then behold there was the old captain who "toed" himself in the shallow water and lifted me across until my feet alighted on the dry strand.*[180]

Captain Charles Joseph Cuevas was well known and well liked in Biloxi, where he operated a pleasure boat called the *Mary C.* for years. All of the visitors to the coast knew Captain Cuevas. He had a reputation of being a very capable sailor with knowledge of all corners of the gulf. He had learned his trade from his father, Captain Louis Cuevas.[181] Louis was also born and raised in Biloxi and was known as one of Biloxi's old-time boatmen. He had sailed in the Mississippi Sound since he was a child. Louis was the son of Charles Ferdinand Cuevas, a son of Juan de Cuevas, the owner of Cat Island. Charles Ferdinand grew up on the family's island, along with his brother and two sisters.[182]

Captain Charles Joseph was raised in his family's home at 704 West Howard Avenue. He was one of four children born to Captain Louis Cuevas and his wife, Marcelline Morin.

On August 2, 1908, Captain Charles Joseph Cuevas married Sarah Westbrook, a native of New Orleans who had moved to the coast when she was fourteen years old. Sarah was twenty-six, and the captain was a year older. Sarah had been previously married to one of the Biloxi Fayards. They had one son, Ambrose Fayard. Other than his name, very little is known of Ambrose or his father.[183] Sarah's family had moved to Biloxi in 1896, although they already had a connection with the coast. Sarah's paternal grandparents were from Ocean Springs, and her maternal grandmother, Sarah Jane Gallagher, had moved to Bay St. Louis in the early 1890s.

No photograph exists of Sarah, but she and her sister, Theresa May Westbrook, shown here, were reported to look very much alike. *Photograph from Find a Grave.*

Sarah's father, Louis Charles Westbrook, and her mother, Henrietta Alverez, were from New Orleans. The couple had eight children, of which Sarah was the second and the oldest daughter.[184]

Life was tragic for the Westbrook family. All but two of the eight Westbrook children died of tuberculosis before the age of twenty-six. The disease also claimed their mother, Henrietta. Ironically, Henrietta Vera Westbrook, the youngest of the children, beat the odds by living to be ninety years old.

By all accounts, Sarah's sister Theresa May Westbrook was an attractive woman who liked to party. The flamboyant Theresa May was a regular at the fireman's hall in

Above: The original casket in which the remains of Sarah Westbrook were discovered was amazingly well preserved. The wood was obviously of high quality. *Photograph by Jason Taylor.*

Left: The tomb of Charles Ferdinand Cuevas, the son of Juan de Cuevas, in the Old Biloxi Cemetery. *Photograph by Chris Cahill.*

Ocean Springs, where she attended the dances that were held there. At one of the balls, she won the title of "most graceful" for her waltz. For most of her life, she apparently lived on the edge. Although she lived to be thirty-two, she never married, but she had two children by two different men. It was said that Sarah Westbrook looked like her sister Theresa May.

Theresa May Westbrook died at her home at 824 Lameuse Street on December 30, 1919, from tuberculosis, the same disease that had killed most of her family. Nothing is known of her financial situation, but according to funeral home records, she was buried in a pauper's grave at the northwest corner of the Biloxi Cemetery, near Irish Hill Street in the new section of the cemetery.

Sarah Westbrook, the wife of Captain Charles Joseph Cuevas and the sister of Theresa May, died of tuberculosis on November 14, 1909, at the age of twenty-seven, just a year after she and Captain Cuevas were married. Then a member of the Cuevas family by marriage, the family allowed Sarah to be buried in the tomb of Juan de Cuevas.

Captain Charles Joseph Cuevas, Sarah's husband, died on August 30, 1918, in Biloxi after a short illness. He was thirty-six years old. He was survived by his mother, Marcelline, and two sisters, Mrs. Chester R. Israel (Lelia) and Miss (Leline) Cuevas. The funeral mass was said in the Church of the Nativity, now the Cathedral of the Nativity of the Blessed Virgin Mary, in Biloxi. Captain Cuevas was buried in his grandfather's, Charles Ferdinand Cuevas's, tomb in the Old Biloxi Cemetery, along with his mother, Marcelline.[185] His sister Lelia Cuevas Israel is buried in a grave with her husband, Chester Rhodes Israel, immediately adjacent to the tomb of Juan de Cuevas, her great-grandfather.[186]

The evidence has shown that Sarah Westbrook Cuevas, as a member of the Cuevas family by marriage, was eligible to be buried in the Juan de Cuevas tomb. Sarah Westbrook Cuevas was the mystery woman.

7

PRESERVATION OF THE OLD BILOXI CEMETERY

By Nick Black

Tombs, like the individuals interred inside, inevitably face a similar fate. The natural process of deterioration affects all aspects of a cemetery. Not only is it a place for people to return to the earth in which they came, it also acts as an ever-changing museum of sorts—one in which decay is permanently on exhibit.

Defined as the process of becoming progressively worse, deterioration is as natural as death and is simply a part of life. Houses, buildings, bridges, any and all structures cannot escape this action. Tombs and monuments are no exception. Deterioration may be classed into two categories: natural and man-made. Natural deterioration is due to nature's effect on materials. For example, moisture and fungi rots and destroys the cellulose that forms wood. Another example is when rainwater or moisture erodes old lime-based mortar. Compared to natural decay, man-made deterioration is a result of human actions. Something as simple as constructing a road next to a structure can directly contribute to this. Whether direct or indirect, everyone plays a part in the process. In some regards, natural deterioration can also be tied to man's own actions.

The lifetime of tombs and monuments is dependent on the quality of construction, the materials used and the environment in which the structure was built. Each aspect is no more important than the next. If construction is subpar, the materials used will not exhibit their full potential within the structure. Furthermore, if a well-built structure utilizes the best of materials but is built in a harsh environment, its service life will be limited when compared to that constructed in an ideal location. With this being said, what was once ideal and perfect may become the complete opposite over a period of time.

As discussed in a previous chapter, many rural cemeteries had tombs developed on an "at need" basis. This was certainly the case in Biloxi. Earlier tombs, such as those constructed during the 1830s and 1840s, were likely built by a family member or a local mason, if one could be found. The majority of burials and interments took place within twenty-four hours after death. As a result, many structures were hastily built. However, it was not uncommon for a body to be interred or temporarily housed until a monument was completed. For a tomb of a simple design, such as platform tombs, this could be done in a matter of a few days.

The Old Biloxi Cemetery faces a common array of conditions that many cemeteries in the South are presented with. Warm, humid air and an abundance of rain contribute to deterioration. This alone has the potential to decay the historic lime mortar that was used to construct many tombs. However, unlike most cemeteries in the South, the Old Biloxi Cemetery is more vulnerable. The location of the graveyard in relation to the shoreline is a significant factor when discussing the rate at which tombs and monuments deteriorate. It should be noted that the landscape is now vastly different from that of the nineteenth century. The coast was once lined with hundreds of trees that bordered the Mississippi Sound. Neither the beach nor Highway 90 existed. Additionally, the cemetery occupied more land to the south than it currently does today. This was discovered in 2018, when a city construction crew accidently unearthed remains within a few feet of Beach Boulevard. The cemetery is now situated less than four hundred feet from the edge of the Gulf of Mexico. Parallel to the artificial beach run two eastbound lanes of the highway. Due north of this is a one-hundred-foot-wide median that surely contains graves that are now long forgotten and have laid unmarked for more than a century.

The low brick-and-iron wall that encloses the cemetery borders the north side of the westbound lanes of Beach Boulevard (Highway 90). Needless to say, the unobstructed view of the gulf makes for a picturesque scene, but this comes at a cost. Tropical weather in the form of storms and, in some cases, severe hurricanes have ravaged the Mississippi coast since its founding. With an elevation of approximately 20 feet above mean sea level, the cemetery sits on fairly high ground. Nevertheless, the storm surge from Hurricane Camille in 1969 reached 24.6 feet, only to be beaten by Hurricane Katrina in 2005, when the surge measured 27.8 feet. During both of these storms, the cemetery received extensive damage. The landscape was turned upside down, tombs were destroyed, headstones laid broken and trees uprooted. It is easy to imagine how one storm of ample strength could have annihilated what once marked the graves of those interred south of the current fence that encloses the south side of the cemetery. Although little history of the cemetery outside of the fence is available, it is reasonable to believe that markers made from stone or wood once covered the area that is now occupied by the median and road. By the time Highway 90 was complete, nothing remained of the southernmost part of the cemetery.

While storms occasionally find their way to the coast, the cemetery has remained idle throughout the decades. Time affects cemeteries in more than one way. As centuries pass, so do the families of those interred there. Neglect of individual plots inevitably leads to a structure's deterioration. Delayed maintenance can be a result of a family moving away or, in some instances, the bloodline dying off. With tombs, it is more likely that the family will continue to use the property well after its construction. This is simply due to the fact that many tombs are designed for unlimited interments; however, this was not always the case. The oldest tombs in the Biloxi Cemetery were constructed for single use. Regardless, there is hardly a tomb that has remained untouched throughout the structure's history. As time goes by and more work is required to maintain or repair a tomb, it is the family's responsibility to see that this occurs. There is often a family member who takes it upon themself to care for the plot. In many instances, homemade repairs, such as cement patchwork, caulking and other simple remedies, would be utilized every few years to keep the tomb visibly acceptable. In the South, this usually occurs before All Saints Day or Easter Sunday. Unfortunately, countless tombs and historical monuments have received irreversible damage due to well-intended maintenance and care throughout the years. Over the last fifty years, the consequences from the use of some materials have been witnessed. With modern products being marketed daily, it is likely this will continue to be an issue. However, it should be noted that there are examples of monuments that are in excellent condition that contradict this. Tombs can be found along the coast that were repaired with materials not intended for application on historic structures, yet they have remained structurally sound. It is important to realize that there are hardly two tombs that have the same maintenance and repair history. Historic materials used, previous repairs and the state of deterioration are all specific details that should be considered when evaluating a structure before restoration.

Biloxi is a fine example of a small town deeply rooted in its history. The same surnames found on the historic tombs situated in the cemetery are still heard around the city today. It is appropriate to suggest that the majority of those interred in the old platform tombs still have descendants residing along the Gulf Coast. With this comes hope that one of these descendants will take the initiative to preserve the resting place of their family. In doing so, they honor those who came before them in addition to securing a physical piece of Biloxi's past for future generations to lay hands on. Currently, the families of both Juan de Cuevas and St. Cyr Zamor (Sancere Seymour) have paid tribute to their ancestors in this way.

RESTORATION OF THE CUEVAS TOMB

During September 2018, my business, NOLA Cemetery Renewal, was contacted by a member of the Descendants of Juan de Cuevas Family Association in regards to the restoration of a tomb in the Old Biloxi Cemetery. Little did I know at this time the historical significance of the family interred in this tomb and that of the structure itself. After several discussions and meetings, my interest grew.

As with any project of this scale, the first step involves a condition assessment survey. During this process, it is critical to thoroughly document the structure as it currently stands. Construction details, condition of the masonry, foundation issues and prior repairs/renovations were all aspects looked into. Oral history of the tomb's past was also recorded. A 3-D scan was taken of the structure in order for a computer-generated model to be created. In doing so, we were able to capture intricate details in the tomb's appearance before any work would begin. As with most condition assessments, testing was not involved which has the potential of being destructive. Due to this, it can be challenging when gauging the exact issues beneath the surface of the structure.

Loose and deteriorated stucco is easily detectible; however, the condition of the brick-and-mortar joints is not always the case. For the Cuevas tomb, little repairs had taken place during the past 150 years. The original stucco was still present; however, it was deteriorated on 80 percent of the structure. The most notable area of decay was found among the two tiers that form the tomb's roof. Stucco had since fallen off, and there was no longer mortar between many of the bricks. Additionally, several bricks were missing. The

Before any work began, the tomb was surveyed, and photographs were taken to document the condition of the tomb and the surrounding site. *Photograph by Chris Cahill.*

only alteration to have occurred throughout the years was found on the front of the tomb—more specifically, the marble closure tablet. During Hurricane Camille, the tablet was ripped from the tomb and broke into several pieces. Mr. Franklin Cuevas, at the time, located the top half of the marble tablet, which contained the inscription of both Juan and Marie. It is assumed that the bottom half of the tablet was either never located or irreparable. Franklin was able to repair the top half by joining the broken segments together. Where the bottom was missing, bricks were used to form a ledge on which to rest the upper half. Due to the deterioration of the material used to connect the broken pieces decades ago, it was necessary to remove the tablet and rejoin it during the restoration.

Following the survey and documentation of the tomb, a scope of work was proposed in addition to the creation of a computer-generated rendering of how the tomb would appear post restoration. Once agreed on by all parties, work began.

The first day at the tomb was spent dismantling all exposed and loose masonry. The structure was sound tested by lightly tapping on the surface with a hammer. A hollow sound when tapped indicates detached stucco, which is then removed. Once the loose stucco was removed, the underlying

Following the survey, a computer-generated rendering was created to show how the tomb would look post restoration. *Photograph by Nick Black.*

On the first day, all loose and deteriorated masonry was removed. *Photograph by Jason Taylor.*

The tomb was sound tested to find areas of delaminated stucco. Each area that had become detached from the brick substrate was recorded and marked. *Photograph by Jason Taylor.*

mortar joints between bricks were inspected. Numerous joints required repointing after the old mortar was raked clean. Like many old structures with stucco, the Cuevas tomb had both major and minor fractures on the surface. Due to the stucco being well adhered in these places, a grinder was used to widen the cracks into a V shape before filling with an appropriate mortar mix. Once the walls of the tomb were determined to be structurally

The majority of the bricks that formed the first and second tier on the roof had to be relayed. This area comprised almost half of the work required to restore the tomb. *Photograph by Jason Taylor.*

An appropriate stucco that is compatible with historic masonry was applied over the bare fire brick that formed the uppermost tier. *Photograph by Jason Taylor.*

sound and all repointing was concluded, the roof was repaired. The Cuevas tomb was constructed from Kendall bricks (also known as Biloxi firebrick). These particular bricks were manufactured between the late 1840s and mid-1850s, approximately the same time the tomb was constructed. Although exceptionally hard, the bricks tend to be brittle. Fortunately, thanks to the kindness of a family friend, enough Kendall bricks were salvaged from outside the cemetery to replace those that were missing. During the roof repair, the top platforms were dismantled. At some point, modern cement stucco was applied over the bare firebrick that formed the uppermost tier. Unlike the original soft lime-based mortar and stucco, this cement encapsulated the bricks, allowing for the top tier to be removed in three large sections. Once off the roof, the cement was grinded away from the bricks so that each unit could be reused. Now that the mortar joints under the two platform tiers were accessible, repointing began. Before the top of the tomb could be reconstructed, a design plan was produced so that the bricks would be re-laid in accordance to the original configuration. This ensured that no mistakes would occur and that all of the bricks were properly utilized. Due to the scarce availability of Kendall bricks, this step was crucial.

Following the reconstruction of the roof tiers, the broken marble frame that surrounds the vault openings was removed, in addition to the closure tablet. Both the tablet and frame were carefully cleaned and rejoined before being installed back onto the tomb. At this point, the tomb was ready to be re-stuccoed. Since the existing stucco was heavily deteriorated, it was necessary to recoat the entire tomb. When built, the finishing coat had vertical and horizontal lines scored through it. This design imitated the ashlar block and gave the appearance that the tomb was constructed from large stone, a feature prominent on many nineteenth-century tombs. Immediately after the new stucco was applied, these lines were scored into it.

The original color of the Cuevas tomb was not known, as nothing remained of what would have been century-old lime washes. Due to the environment the tomb is subject to and the desired longevity of a coating, a mineral paint was used as the finish. This specific paint is breathable, highly durable, mildew resistant and perfectly compatible for use on historic masonry.

Several photographs of the Cuevas tomb from the mid-twentieth century exist. In nearly each photograph, a brick walkway around the tomb is noticeable. Without knowledge of a path once existing, no one

Above: Any Portland cement patches that had been used in previous repairs were carefully removed. *Photograph by Jason Taylor.*

Left: The marble closure tablet and frame were repaired and reinstalled on the tomb. *Photograph by Chris Cahill.*

Opposite, top: The entire tomb required an overlay of new stucco. *Photograph by Chris Cahill.*

Opposite, bottom: A mineral-based coating suitable for historic masonry was applied to the tomb. *Photograph by Jason Taylor.*

Above: The finishing coat had vertical and horizontal lines scored through it. This imitated the ashlar blocks that were prominent on many nineteenth-century tombs. *Photograph by Jason Taylor.*

would have known about it when looking at the tomb pre-restoration. It was discovered that the original brick walkway was still present; however, it was covered by six to eight inches of soil. Once this soil was removed, the majority of the Kendall bricks were safely excavated. Crushed rock was used as a fill material, and the site was graded. There were no indications of the original walkway having mortared joints; however, the new walkway would have them. Following the cleaning and re-laying of the bricks, a cement border was formed parallel to the front and rear edges of the path. This border now prevents bricks from slipping away, as they had previously done.

To complete the project, two additions were installed on the tomb, the first being a marble cross that the family association requested be placed on the roof. Although it is not known whether a cross originally adorned the structure, it was nonetheless a fitting touch that does not permanently alter the structure in any way. In order to keep the proper aesthetics, an

Left: The original walkway bricks were excavated from several inches of soil and were salvaged and reused for the new walkway. *Photograph by Jason Taylor.*

Below: The old bricks were laid in the same pattern as that of the original walkway. *Photograph by Chris Cahill.*

Opposite: A descriptive plaque was attached to the rear of the restored tomb in honor of Juan de Cuevas the "Hero of Cat Island." *Photograph by Jason Taylor.*

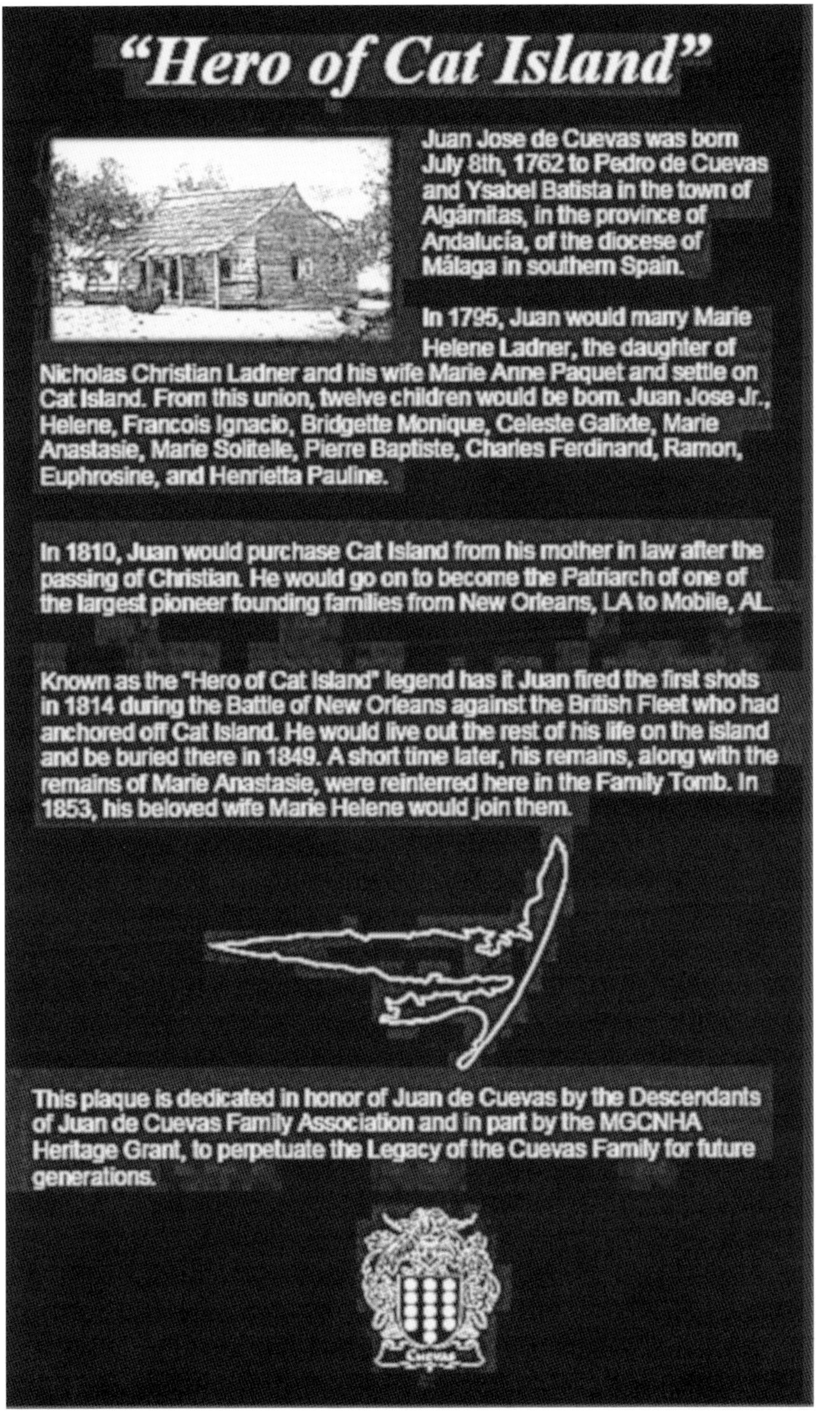
"Hero of Cat Island"
Juan Jose de Cuevas was born July 8th, 1762 to Pedro de Cuevas and Ysabel Batista in the town of Algámitas, in the province of Andalucía, of the diocese of Málaga in southern Spain.
In 1795, Juan would marry Marie Helene Ladner, the daughter of Nicholas Christian Ladner and his wife Marie Anne Paquet and settle on Cat Island. From this union, twelve children would be born. Juan Jose Jr., Helene, Francois Ignacio, Bridgette Monique, Celeste Galixte, Marie Anastasie, Marie Solitelle, Pierre Baptiste, Charles Ferdinand, Ramon, Euphrosine, and Henrietta Pauline.
In 1810, Juan would purchase Cat Island from his mother in law after the passing of Christian. He would go on to become the Patriarch of one of the largest pioneer founding families from New Orleans, LA to Mobile, AL.
Known as the "Hero of Cat Island" legend has it Juan fired the first shots in 1814 during the Battle of New Orleans against the British Fleet who had anchored off Cat Island. He would live out the rest of his life on the island and be buried there in 1849. A short time later, his remains, along with the remains of Marie Anastasie, were reinterred here in the Family Tomb. In 1853, his beloved wife Marie Helene would join them.
This plaque is dedicated in honor of Juan de Cuevas by the Descendants of Juan de Cuevas Family Association and in part by the MGCNHA Heritage Grant, to perpetuate the Legacy of the Cuevas Family for future generations.
Cuevas

An 1850s marble cross is placed on top of the completed tomb. *Photograph by Jason Taylor.*

1850s marble cross was secured and donated to the association for use on the tomb. Following this addition, a memorial plaque was furnished and installed on the rear wall of the tomb. The plaque reads:

> *Known as the "Hero of Cat Island" it is said that in 1814, Juan fired the first shots during the Battle of New Orleans against the British Fleet who had anchored off the Island. He would live out the rest of his life on the Island and be buried there in 1849. A short time later, his remains, along with the remains of Marie Anastasie, were reinterred here in the tomb. In 1853, his beloved wife Marie Helene would join them.*

8

THE REDEDICATION CEREMONY

On June 22, 2019, the Descendants of Juan de Cuevas Family Association hosted the Juan de Cuevas Rededication Memorial Ceremony at the Old Biloxi Cemetery in recognition of the newly restored tomb of Juan de Cuevas and his wife, Marie. An estimated seventy-five people were in attendance, several of whom had traveled from as far away as Jacksonville, Florida. Reenactors in period costumes presented a twenty-one-gun salute to Juan and Marie. Draped behind the soldiers were the flags of Spain, the United States and the official flag of the Juan de Cuevas Family Association. In the distance, a cannon was fired to highlight the proceedings. The weather was clear but hot and muggy, making the 90 degrees Fahrenheit feel like 107 degrees Fahrenheit. Fortunately, much of the old section of the cemetery is draped by mighty oak trees that sheltered the young and old who had come to pay their respects.

Speakers included the association's president Dorty Necaise, who gave an introduction, followed by Deron Cuevas and Michael Hoda, who spoke about the renovation of the tomb and an overview of the family association. Nick Black of New Orleans Cemetery Renewals described his unique profession, his involvement with the restoration and some of the steps he took in bringing the old tomb back to its original appearance. Historian and author John Cuevas gave a brief history of how Juan de Cuevas had arrived on the coast from his native Spain and the impact

Reenactors in period costumes were present during the rededication ceremony. Seen here are Dorty Necaise and Tammy Henzen; both are Cuevas descendants. *Photograph by Chris Cahill.*

Right: Men in period costumes fired vintage rifles in a tribute to Juan de Cuevas and his wife, Marie. *Photograph by Chris Cahill.*

Below: Cuevas descendant Daryl Ladner fired a cannon to highlight the proceedings. *Photograph by Chris Cahill.*

Descendants of Juan de Cuevas Family Association president Dorty Necaise gave the opening introduction. *Photograph by Chris Cahill.*

that the Cuevas family of Juan de Cuevas has had on the Gulf Coast. Bill Raymond of Biloxi Main Street (a nonprofit organization) accepted the grant on behalf of the Descendants of Juan de Cuevas Family Association, and Jeff Rosenberg Department of Marine Resources/Mississippi Gulf Coast National Heritage Area was acknowledged for making the grant possible.

A solemn service followed, with the laying of wreaths at the base of the tomb in commemoration of each of the twelve Cuevas children. A special wreath from the association was placed at the entrance of the tomb, along with a floral arrangement in memory of the unknown female who had been discovered during the restoration process, also buried in the Cuevas

Tammy Henzen depicted Juan's wife, Marie, during the ceremony. *Photograph by Chris Cahill.*

Above: Wreaths were laid at the base of the tomb, commemorating each of the twelve Cuevas children. A special wreath in honor of Juan and Marie Cuevas was placed at the entrance to the tomb. *Photograph by Chris Cahill.*

Left: Father Dennis Carver, pastor of the Cathedral of the Nativity of the Blessed Virgin Mary in Biloxi, offered the opening prayer before blessing the newly restored tomb. *Photograph by Chris Cahill.*

tomb. One of the Cuevas descendants, Susan Necaise, had painstakingly handmade all of the wreaths for the ceremony. Father Dennis Carver, the pastor of the Cathedral of the Nativity of the Blessed Virgin Mary in Biloxi, offered the opening prayer before blessing the newly restored tomb. News anchor Mike Lacy of Biloxi's WLOX-TV covered the proceedings.

Appendix

THE CUEVAS FAMILY OF CAT ISLAND

It was not so remarkable that Juan de Cuevas and his wife, Marie Ladner, had twelve children; after all, large families were very common in rural areas in the eighteenth and nineteenth centuries. The remarkable thing about the Cuevas family is the impact that these children had on the Mississippi Gulf Coast—more so than any other family, regardless of size. Hancock County historian Charles Gray once explained the phenomenon, "Nicholas Ladner had 12 children. One daughter (Marie Helene) married Juan de Cuevas and from them are 63,000 descendants." Almost every one of the old families can trace their roots back to Cat Island and to one of the children or grandchildren of this remarkable couple. These names, including Ladner, Lizana, Seymour, Nicaise, Dedeaux, Garriga, Garcia, Guardia, Moran, Krohn, Caillavet, Fountain, Favre, Guardia, Basquez, Mauffrey, Foretich, Dubuisson, Malley, Fayard, Carcaux, Cronier, Hoda, Gollotte, Fournier, Penalver, Hale, Northrop, Saucier, Niolet, Peterson, Stiglets, Cameron, Creel, Balius, Delaunay, Yarborough, Fornea, Cruthirds, Letort, Boggs, Curet and many more, have branches on the Cuevas family tree. It was not uncommon for each of these families to have between ten and fourteen children each, and the children, in turn, had equal numbers. With the quantity of family members increasing exponentially and the population of the area being so sparse, it was almost impossible not to marry into the Cuevas clan.

No photographs of Juan de Cuevas, Marie or any of their twelve children will ever be found because none exist. The process of photography had barely

The first image of a human being in a photograph. *Public Domain.*

been discovered during their lifetimes. Louis-Jacques-Mande Daguerre (November 18, 1787–July 10, 1851) first went public with his invention, the daguerreotype, on August 13, 1839.[187] Before that time, photography was an undreamed-of piece of science fiction. The families on Cat Island had no idea such a miracle existed. While photography was eventually available in the late 1840s, this new process did not reach Cat Island and the rural area of the coast for well over a decade.

A year after his invention was announced, Daguerre took the first photograph of a human being, titled *Boulevard du Temple* (Paris, 1838). In this historic photograph, the panoramic picture of the boulevard seems to be completely disserted, except for one lone individual who was standing on a corner brushing his boots.[188] The anonymous man appears as a small fuzzy shape dwarfed by large buildings. While he appears to be alone, the street was actually bustling with cars and people going about their daily lives, but they were moving too fast to be captured due to the long exposure necessary for the early photographic process. Only this one man stood stationary long enough to be immortalized on film.

The blurred figure in that first photograph, whose grainy form is hardly recognizable, was once a real person, but if it were not for this incredible image, the world would never have known this man ever existed. One man singled out, standing on the corner of a boulevard, unaware that he was captured in time. Who was he? Where was he going? We will never know.

Before photography, portrait painting was the only means of capturing someone's likeness. Since portrait painting required considerable training, expensive materials and long sittings, it was only available to the wealthy. The new science of photography was an opportunity—at last—for the middle class to attain affordable portraits of their family and friends. As with any new discovery or invention, it takes time to become commonly available. In the beginning, only persons specially trained by Daguerre himself were able to master this new art. Mathew Brady, one of the early pioneer photographers, took the first ever photograph of a U.S. president, President James Polk (1795–1849), on February 14, 1849, the year Juan de Cuevas died.[189]

Old photographs tempt us with the possibility that we might discover what the world was like in a previous era. Sadly, the past can never fully be recovered. I am reminded of the scripture, "Life is like a vapor that lingers in the air a moment and then vanishes away forever."[190]

While genealogy is an entertaining and rewarding hobby that is currently enjoying great popularity, it has never satisfied my longing to really know the people. A newly discovered leaf on the family tree is never the real person, rather, it is nothing more than a name scrawled on a piece of paper. Like working a crossword puzzle, one simply fills in the blanks with words, not faces. Since we have neither photographs nor paintings of the original Cuevas family, we can only imagine what these people must have looked like. We don't even have a vague shape like the man in the Paris photograph that would give us the slightest hint as to their appearances.

Since we have no early photographs, I wanted to learn as much as I could about the people themselves. As a child, I listened intently to my grandmother and others of her age tell about the "old folks." She was a contemporary of some of Juan's children and the last connection we had to our precious past. Now that my grandmother and her generation are long gone, I am left with only the wonderful memories of our many conversations. Even as a young boy, I could sense the significance of their knowledge, and I made a diligent effort to listen and to learn as much as I could about the family.

While the following details of each individual are sketchy at best, I have pieced together the information we have about each of the members of the original Cuevas family to make up for our lack of photographs. I have attempted to breathe life into these once-living souls. While my effort is not anything as comprehensive or accurate as I would like it to be, the following is probably as close as we will ever come to knowing the Cuevas family of Cat Island.

MARIE HELENE LADNER MATRIARCH OF THE CUEVAS FAMILY

Marie Helen Ladner was born in 1775 on Cat Island to Nicholas Christian Ladner and Marianne Paquet.[191] About a year before she was born, her father, the man for whom Pass Christian would later be named, moved from Bayou St. John in New Orleans and began living permanently on Cat Island, where he had been bringing cattle for years. At that time, the islands in the Mississippi Sound were being used as cattle pasturage.[192]

On February 10, 1763, the Treaty of Paris was signed by the kingdoms of Great Britain, France and Spain. In the treaty, Great Britain gained many of France's possessions in North America, including the eastern half of French Louisiana—that is, the area from the Mississippi River to the Appalachian Mountains, including the Mississippi Gulf Coast.[193] In 1764, Nicholas Ladner visited Mobile to take an oath of allegiance to Great Britain. While there, he registered his claim to Cat Island with the British (2,978 acres).[194]

In 1781, before the British acted on Ladner's claim, the coast came under the control of Spain.[195] On August 1, 1781, the Spanish honored Nicholas Ladner's request for a grant to Cat Island, a request he had made to the British seventeen years earlier.[196] This made Ladner the first ever private owner of Cat Island.

In 1784, a small group of Spanish troops from the fort in Pensacola was garrisoned on Cat Island. Juan de Cuevas, age twenty-two, was one of these soldiers.[197] During this time, Cuevas met the Ladner family. When Juan left the military, he settled permanently on Deer Island. It wasn't long before Juan also began keeping cattle on Cat Island. Since he visited the island often, he eventually fell in love with Ladner's young daughter Marie Helene. In 1785, Nicholas Ladner built the house for his family on Cat Island that, in later years, became known as the "Cuevas Place."[198] In 1794, Juan de Cuevas, age thirty-two, married the nineteen-year-old Marie Helene Ladner.[199]

On June 3, 1788, Spain granted Nicholas Ladner's request for land on the mainland at what is now part of Long Beach and West Gulfport.[200] Ladner and his family moved to his new property, where he lived until his death circa 1799.[201] The property became known as "Old Chimneys" because of the dogtrot house he built with two large chimneys that could be seen from long distances at sea.[202] The chimneys were used as navigational tools for ships passing through the channel to New Orleans. The two chimneys survived long after the house itself was eventually destroyed.

After Juan and Marie married, they moved into Juan's original home on Deer Island. After the birth of at least four of their children, the couple moved into the Ladner family home on Cat Island. On July 4, 1810, Juan de Cuevas bought Cat Island from his mother-in-law, who was a widow at that time, for a total of $160. Thus began the legacy of the Cuevas family on Cat Island.

Marie was the perfect wife and mother. The size and strength of all the family was a testament to her good cooking. She believed the old adage that cleanliness was next to godliness, and she saw to it that the modest Cuevas home was kept immaculately straight, making sure that even the slightest grain of sand was swept through the cracks in the house's wooden floor. She was also a very kind and caring person. Her grandson James tells of how she tenderly cared for the captain whose boat had been commandeered by pirates. She cradled the injured man's head in her lap and gently fed him homemade soup one spoonful at a time.

Like most of the other French and Spanish immigrants, religion was important to her and to Juan. Together, they saw to it that the children were raised as devout Catholics, though they saw a priest only on occasion. She taught them all the prayers and saw to it that they were recited daily. Family was very important to Juan and Marie, and the children learned that to survive in such a harsh environment, family meant everything. Even though they were not educated, Marie taught the children manners and respect for their elders. All of the Cuevas children grew up to be outstanding citizens and contributors to the emerging Gulf Coast community.

Marie died on October 10, 1853, at the age of seventy-eight, only four years after the death of her husband.[203] Both she and Juan had lived to a very old age, considering the lack of available medicine at the time and the hard life they led as pioneers on a wild and untamed coast.

The traditional wake was also conducted for Marie. After the perfunctory three days, her funeral service was held at the Cuevas home. Marie was buried on Cat Island next to her husband while the new family fault was being built in the Old Biloxi Cemetery. After the tomb was completed, her body, along with Juan's, was then disinterred on Cat Island and transported to the Biloxi Cemetery, where it was to be placed in the new family vault. Although it has always been believed that the Cuevas vault only held the bodies of Juan and Marie, it was recently discovered during the restoration of the tomb (in 2019) that is also contained the body of their child Marie Anastasie. Anastasie had died somewhere around the age of five. She was the only one of the couple's twelve children who did not live to adulthood.

It was common for small, two-vault tombs to be used for the interment of several family members over time.[204] Since Juan and Anastasie had been buried for a while, what was left of their remains was placed together in the bottom of the tomb. The casket containing Marie's body was then slid into the vault in the top position.

The decision to also remove the body of Anastasie came after the marble tablet at the entrance of the tomb had already been placed. Only Juan and Marie's names, therefore, are chiseled on the marble slab. When a mystery lady was buried in the vault some sixty years later, Marie's remains were moved to the bottom with Juan and Anastasie. The coffin containing the young lady's remains was placed on the top shelf. The entrance was sealed permanently, and the marble slab was replaced. The young lady's name was not added on the tablet.

THE CUEVAS CHILDREN

Juan José de Cuevas II (John Joseph Cuevas)

Juan José de Cuevas II was born in 1796, while the family was still living on Deer Island.[205] He was the first child born in the Cuevas family. Juan could not have been prouder, and as one would expect, the baby was named after his father. Since the label "Jr." is not used in Spanish, both the father and son shared the same full name. To distinguish between the two, Juan and Marie called their small son "Juanito," meaning "little Juan" in Spanish.[206]

Like the other children who were born on the coast at that time, Juanito had no formal education. There was no real need to read or write, as it was more important for the children to learn skills that would help them survive in the harsh environment in which they lived. Juanito testified that he was illiterate in a deposition he gave on August 12, 1848. In the document, he stated, "I am 53 years old....I cannot read or write...and I do not know much about the title of lands." His parents taught him to be an honest, hardworking man, instilling in him, as well as his brothers and sisters, strong moral values.

Even without a formal education, John Joseph became a resourceful young man. He had a strong sense of loyalty to his family, often putting their needs above his own. He valued tradition and was very conservative in his approach to life. Although he was just a laborer by trade, he was methodical in anything he did and was usually working on several jobs simultaneously.

In 1818, at the age of twenty-two, John Joseph married Eugenie "Gena" Ladner, the daughter of Jean Baptiste Ladner II and Francoise Baudrau.[207] The couple's first child, Josephine Antoinette, was born on June 14, 1820. The family called the little girl Josephina.[208] John Joseph and Gena eventually had seven children. In addition to Josephina, the others were Eugenie, Juan José III, Zenon, Sylvain, Simon and Romain. Sometime after the birth of their last child, Romain, the family moved to Biloxi.[209]

While living in Biloxi, John Joseph's son Juan José Cuevas III lived on one side of him, while his son Zenon, or "Zeno," lived on the other.[210] His family was always very close, both physically and emotionally. When he moved in 1860 to the general area of what is now Cuevas, Mississippi, his children Juan III, Romain and Simon followed him.[211]

According to his family, John Joseph had problems with his legs and knees, being prone to rheumatism or some form of arthritis. We don't know the cause or the exact date of his death, but we do know that he lived a long and full life. Juan José Cuevas II was buried in the Wolf River Cemetery.

Helene Cuevas

Helene Cuevas, the second child of Juan and Marie, was born on Deer Island on October 1, 1797.[212] Helene was named after her mother and called Elena by her parents. By all accounts, Elena was probably the prettiest of the Cuevas girls. She was tall and moved with elegance and grace. Like most of the Cuevas family, she was a naturally kind and gentle person. Even as a child, she was very sensitive to others.

Elena was surprisingly energetic, although it was no secret that she disliked dirty work. Like her brother Juanito, she was probably spoiled, since they were the first two children born to Juan and Marie. More than any of her sisters, she was very conscious of what she wore and displayed a sense of fashion, although limited by her environment.

Elena was about twenty years old when she and her sister Bridget began dating two Ladner boys. She was infatuated by Julian, who, at the time, was only seventeen. Julian was three years younger than Elena.[213] His father, Jean Baptiste Ladner II, and mother, Françoise Carcaux, tried to discourage the relationship at first, but the young couple convinced them that the difference in their ages would have no effect on their relationship. At the same time that Elena and Julian were dating, Bridget was also falling in love with Julian's brother Jean Baptiste III. Bridget married Jean Baptiste on January 30, 1820, and Elena married Julian a month later, on February 4, in New Orleans.[214]

Elena and Julian made their home on the eastern bank of the Jordan River on 582 acres of land, sold to them by Julian's father, Jean Baptiste Ladner II. The land was part of his father's original land grant. The land had first been settled by Julian's grandfather Jean Baptiste Ladner and his grandmother Marie Louise Fisseau dit DeLorme.[215]

Elena and Julian had a large family of fourteen children. Their first child was a boy, whom they named after Julian. He was the first grandchild born to Juan de Cuevas and Marie. The other children were: Adele, Adeline, Leandre (called Leon), Zeline, Celestine, Jean (called Juanille), Raymond, Louis Vital, Edmond, Edwin, Georgina, Roseline and Marie Aurelie.

The Ladner family and the Cuevas family were always closely intertwined. Not only did Elena's younger sister Bridget Cuevas marry Julian's brother Jean Baptiste Ladner III, but their daughter Adeline married her own first cousin Narcisse Simon "Semore" Ladner, the son of Gilbert Ladner and Louise Desiree "Pouponne" Morin.[216] Gilbert was the son of Julien Ladner II and his wife, Clementine Ladner.

No one knows when Elena died, but we can assume she lived at least to middle age and beyond. Although she was in decent health, she was not without some issues. As she got older, she complained of back problems. Today, it would probably be diagnosed as lumbago or possibly some form of kidney disease. She could well have had kidney stones. It is uncertain if these problems eventually led to her death, but we know that she was buried in the Rotten Bayou Cemetery.

François Ignace Cuevas

François Ignace Cuevas was born on Deer Island in 1799.[217] He was the third child born to Juan de Cuevas and Marie. Of all of the children,

François was the most religious. Even as a child, he seemed to have a strong sense of morality. Catholicism fit perfectly with his temperament. In fact, he adhered so strictly to the ritual codes of the church that his family often felt that he was more interested in the rituals than the belief in God. But no one could deny that he was sincerely a good person. Even as a young man, he was very responsible when looking after the elderly members of the Ladner family.

François married Felicite Morin, the daughter of Pierre Morin and Judith Nicaise.[218] The family made their home on the Jordan River. The couple had a long and prosperous life together, raising a family of twelve children. The children were: Francois II, Onezine (called "Lezan"), Euphrosine, Lucien, Ursin, Susan, Rosemond, Marie Delouise, John, Cyrille (called "Saula") and the twins, Armand and Armantine. This was the first of several sets of twins who have been born in the Cuevas family. In fact, twins are very common within the family.

Three of François's children married their first cousins. His oldest child, François Ignace II, married Marie "Mary" Morin, the daughter of Pierre Morin and Marie Nicasise; his son Lezan married Mathilde Morin, the daughter of Lucien Morin and Henriette Nicaise; and his daughter Euphrosine married Jean "Joanille" Ladner.[219] Joanille was the son of Julian Ladner and Elena Cuevas, his father's sister.

François died January 28, 1863, in Hancock County.[220] The children buried him on the family property. When their mother died twenty-seven years later, on August 20, 1890, she was buried next to François. The children inherited their family's property, and as a fitting tribute to their parents, they donated the land to Hancock County to establish a community cemetery. The cemetery was dedicated on August 7, 1893, and became known as the Rotten Bayou Cemetery, now in the Diamondhead community.[221] Both François and his wife were buried there, along with his older sister Elena and other family members. Today, the cemetery is known as the St. Joseph Cemetery, named after the Catholic church nearby.

Bridget Monique Cuevas

Bridget Monique Cuevas was born on March 4, 1800.[222] She was the fourth of the children to be born on Deer Island. Bridget was easygoing and affectionate. Everyone loved her because she was so compassionate and sensitive to the feelings of others.

Bridget loved her Ladner grandparents and spent many days at their home at the Chimneys in what is now Long Beach. Ever since her older sister, Elena, had been dating Julian Ladner, Bridget had been infatuated with Julian's older brother. Jean Baptiste III, who was only two years older than Bridget, was living in Bay St. Louis at the time. Both girls would take every opportunity to see the boys. The two couples were always close. The boys also liked the Old Chimneys community and would visit the Ladner home, usually when they knew the girls would be there. Fate seemed to bring the two couples together. A romance began and on January 30, 1820, when Bridget married Jean Baptiste Ladner III.[223] A month later, her older sister, Elena, married his brother Julian.

After their wedding, Jean Baptiste purchased land in the Old Chimneys settlement from their uncle Claude Ladner, the son of Nicholas Ladner and Marianne.[224] They lived their entire lives on this land and raised a family of eleven children. The first children born were twins, Celeste and Jean Baptiste IV. The boy apparently never married. His twin sister, Celeste, however, married Jean Baptiste Cronier, a native of France, when she was only seventeen. Jean Cronier was fifteen years older than Celeste.

Bridget's other children were Celestin, Charles Lovance, Euphemie Francine, Euphrosine (called Frazina), Pierre, Celestine, Clementine, Raymond Eugene and Remy. All of the children were raised at the Old Chimneys, although the family moved temporarily to the other side of Lake Ponchartrain, where Jean Baptiste had taken a job. While they were there, their son Celestin was born. He was baptized on Decemeber 16, 1825, at St. Louis Cathedral in New Orleans, with his uncle Francois and aunt Felicite as his godparents.[225] When the job ended in New Orleans, Jean Baptiste and the family anxiously moved back to their home at the Old Chimneys.

Bridget's daughter Clementine married Salathiel Smith on March 14, 1854, and raised nine children in the Long Beach area.[226] When the post office was established at Mississippi City on March 31, 1854, Salathiel was appointed as the first postmaster. He served in that position until August 9, 1854, when a successor was appointed.[227] The distance between the Old Chimneys and Mississippi City was too great to make the job practical.

Clementine and her son Lovance, who was born in 1860, would be interviewed in 1907 by a reporter for the *Times-Picayune* newspaper. They became the first published details of the legend of Juan de Cuevas and the Battle of New Orleans. Bridget died on March 22, 1897, in Long Beach, Mississippi. Her husband, Jean Baptiste, had been dead since 1851.[228] It is believed that she is buried in the Rotten Bayou Cemetery.

Celeste Galixte Cuevas

In 1803, Celeste Galixte Cuevas was born on Deer Island. She was baptized on June 12 of that same year in Mobile, Alabama.[229]

Celeste had a strong and attractive personality, although it is said that she was somewhat of a loner. The truth is that she was a very sensitive, gentle and patient person who liked her "quiet time." This was often misinterpreted by the family. Everyone agreed, however, that she was always intelligent, concise, clear and logical. She had a reputation for being fiercely independent, refusing to go along with the crowd. Gines Garcia was attracted to her forthcoming and open personality. Gines had arrived on the coast from Cartavena de DeVante, Spain, and mixed easily with the other Spaniards in the community. Although Juan de Cuevas was about twenty years older than Celeste, Ramon Garriga and Gines Garcia were often visitors to Cat Island.[230] Juan's daughter Celeste was attracted to this dark, handsome man from Spain. Their romance developed, and they were married on December 16, 1825.[231]

The newly married couple made their home on Cat Island. The Garcias had a family of seven children. The children were: Marie Isabelle, Ferdinand, Clarisse Adelaide, Joseph Manuel, Anne, Manuel and Eugene. In 1833, after the birth of their fourth child, Joseph Manuel, they purchased land from Celeste's uncle Claude Christian Ladner, and the family moved to the Old Chimneys settlement on the mainland.[232] They lived there for twenty years on their land at Old Chimneys before selling it to Dr. William H. Teagarden on August 4, 1853.[233]

Dr. Teagarden had married Susan McCaughan, the daughter of John Johnston McCaughan. John McCaughan was a surveyor and civil engineer. When he first came to the coast, he settled at what is now Mississippi City. He amassed a fortune in real estate, becoming the largest landowner on the coast, with the exception of Marianne Ladner, the widow of Nicholas Christian and the mother of Juan's wife, Marie. Later, McCaughan purchased a part of the widow Ladner's land from her son Claude. He built a beautiful home on the site of the present-day University of Southern Mississippi, Gulf Park campus. He called his home "Rosalie," possibly after Fort Rosalie, which was built by the French in 1716 in Natchez, Mississippi. Dr. Teagarden and his father-in-law were later instrumental in the construction of the historic St. Marks Episcopal Church in Mississippi City in 1855.

After Gines and Celeste sold their property at Old Chimneys, they moved to the area now known as Lakeshore, just west of Waveland. After the

Hancock County census of 1850, there is no record of Gines. He apparently died before the next census, as Celeste is listed as a widow. At the time of the 1870 census, Celeste was living with her son Ferdinand, who was forty-five at the time. Her son Joseph was living next door to her and Ferdinand.

On June 19, 1880, Celeste and her children sold a part of their land at Lakeshore, but even today, the Garcia family considers Lakeshore their home. We have no information on when Celeste died, but it is possible that she was buried in the Rotten Bayou Cemetery.

Marie Anastasie Cuevas

Marie Anastasie Cuevas was born on Deer Island in 1805. Almost nothing else is known about this little Cuevas girl. It is a common practice in Spanish-speaking countries to use the parents' first names for their same-sex children. This is why two of the Cuevas daughters were named after their mother: Marie Anastasie and Marie Solitelle. Marie was baptized on December 8, 1805, at the Church of the Immaculate Conception in Mobile.[234] Records—or rather, the lack of records—indicate that she died at a very young age.[235] She was buried on Cat Island and later moved to the Cuevas tomb in the Old Biloxi Cemetery to be with her parents.

Marie Solitelle Cuevas

Marie Solitelle Cuevas was born sometime in 1807, about two years after Anastasie was born. From all accounts, Marie Solitelle possessed a hypnotic personality. Her eyes were her most outstanding feature. Described as penetrating, they could make you feel as if she was looking straight into your soul.

They say Marie Solitelle was brooding at times but often volatile. This appealed to the young German Henry Krohn. Heinrich Auguste Krohn was born in Hamburg, Germany, on March 9, 1802. Henry was twenty-five when he arrived at the port of Philadelphia on a ship from Bordeaux, France. From there, he sailed to the port of New Orleans, arriving in Louisiana on July 9, 1827. From the moment the couple met, they knew they were meant to be together. On November 16, 1829, they were married by Reverend Louis Moni, the pastor of St. Louis Cathedral, and took up residence on Cat Island.[236]

Three years later, in 1832, they moved to Biloxi, where they purchased land from Francois Bouquet to build their home.[237] The property was quite large, measuring 720 feet along the beachfront and 7,680 feet deep, extending all the way to Back Bay.[238] They lived there until 1837, when they sold the property to Jacob Elmer and moved to land on the Tchoutacabouffa River. Their land on the river was an 80-acre plot that Henry purchased in September 1842 from Louis A. Caillavet and his wife, Margaret.[239] Three years later, Solitelle's father, Juan de Cuevas, gave the couple 160 acres next to their home.[240] He had received the property as a land grant on January 5, 1841, and donated it to Solitelle.

During the time that he owned this property, Henry farmed the land, growing vegetables, pecan trees and fruit trees. He was also becoming very active and prominent in Biloxi's city government. He became the first supervisor of District No. 1 Harrison County Board of Supervisors, what was then called the Board of Police. He was elected president of that body on November 22, 1841. During his term as president, he spearheaded the building of a jail and courthouse. In addition to the construction of roads connecting the towns within the county, he also oversaw the establishment of two ferries. He served as the president until 1843, after which time, he served as the inspector of elections in the third district. In 1847, he was an interpreter for the probate court.[241]

Solitelle and Henry had ten children. The first two children, John Henry and Charles F., were born while the family still lived on Cat Island. The other children: Marie Elizabeth, Louise, Robert Vincent, Louis Henry, Edward Albert, Bridget Eleanor and Caroline Virginia where born in Biloxi.

By 1861, the Civil War was beginning to affect the lives of many of the coast's residents. Several young men of the Cuevas family were pressed into service to help the Southern cause. The Mississippi volunteers were mostly farmers who had never traveled far from their fields. The war offered them an exciting experience, and many eagerly joined in the effort. While the ages of the men ranged from the youngest teen to graying men who were hardly able to carry their rifles, all were ready to fight to protect their families and their way of life.

Solitelle's son Louis Henry joined the Handsboro, Company E, Adams Rifles on May 20, 1861. Later, he was transferred to Loring's Division, Twentieth Regiment, CSA, which fought in the war alongside the Third Mississippi Infantry Regiment. Another son, Charles, joined company A, the Live Oak Rifles, of the Third Mississippi Regiment four months later, even though he had married Sarah A. Cruthird five years before joining. There is a possibility that Louis was killed in the war, since there are no further records of him. Charles, on the other hand, returned home in July 1863.

Henry Auguste Krohn died peacefully on October 11, 1861. His funeral was quite large, with many family members, friends and city officials attending. The children buried their father on property that was thought to be owned by Charles, but apparently, that was not the case. Charles had purchased 240 acres in Harrison County at a state swampland sale on May 29, 1858. He purchased an additional 40 acres in January 1859 from Alexander Scarborough. The family thought that they had buried Henry on the Krohn property, but as it turned out, Henry was buried just sixteen feet west of Charles's property line. Mr. J.J. McCaughan of Mississippi City actually owned the land on which the grave was located. McCaughan had purchased the land from the Harrison County School Board in 1851.[242]

One of the Krohn's children was either physically or mentally challenged. Solitelle's daughter Bridget was apparently born with some defect or was otherwise incapacitated. Although we don't really know her condition, Bridget was never expected to marry, and it seems she would have required some special care for the rest of her life. For ten years after the death of her husband, Henry, Solitelle looked after Bridget with the help of the other children. But in 1861, Solitelle knew that she herself was dying. Solitelle was concerned about who would take care of Bridget and her youngest daughter, Caroline, who was then only fourteen, after she passed away.

Pierre Cuevas, Solitelle's younger brother, had given Solitelle an enslaved girl named Ann and her infant son, Louis, several years before. Solitelle eventually sold Ann but kept Louis. Louis grew to be a strong, healthy eighteen-year-old mulatto boy and an enslaved man for life.

On February 20, 1861, two months before her death, Solitelle prepared a legal document that put her son Charles in charge of a trust that would ensure the well-being of Bridget for the rest of her life. The document gave Charles ownership of her young enslaved boy, Louis, to her son Charles F. Krohn, with the stipulation that two-thirds of the money earned by Louis was to be paid annually by Charles to Bridget. The remaining one-third was to be paid to Caroline, as long as she remained single and did not marry. This was not intended to keep Caroline single; it was only to ensure that she was cared for until she had a husband to look after her. If Caroline were to die before she married, the full proceeds earned by Louis were to revert to Bridget. When Bridget died, the money would be divided between Solitelle's heirs.[243]

Marie Solitelle Cuevas Krohn died on July 18, 1861. After her death, Caroline went to live with her older sister Marie Elizabeth and her husband, Edwin R. Latimer. Bridget lived a for few more years after her mother's death, but we are not sure exactly how long. Her name does not show up on the Jackson County census of 1870, so we know that she was dead before that year. Caroline grew up and married Narcisse Seymour on September 18, 1873.

Solitelle's son Charles, who had been left in charge of the two girls' well-being, died on March 28, 1876, and was buried on his property near his father. His burial started what is now called the Krohn Family Cemetery. The cemetery now lies on public land and is maintained by the Harrison County Board of Supervisors, the same board of which Henry was the first member.

Solitelle was reportedly buried in a private cemetery in Biloxi in the Sunkist development.

Pierre Baptiste Cuevas

Pierre Baptiste Cuevas was born on Deer Island in 1809.[244] Pierre, who was called Perrique by the family, was the most dominant, spontaneously creative and extroverted of all of his brothers and sisters. Although he became the most controversial of the Cuevas children, he left a legacy in the North Biloxi area that continues to this day. Not only were he and his children very successful in business, but Pierre's family is the origin of the Quave name on the Gulf Coast.

Perrique never met a stranger, and he took every opportunity to make sure he was noticed. Even as a small child, he was strong-willed and self-confident. He was probably the most intelligent of the Cuevas children and often proved to be a handful for his parents. Although there was hardly any need for schooling in the wilderness that existed in those days, Pierre understood the importance of learning to read and write. Along with his younger brother, Charles Ferdinand, they became the only two of Juan's children with the ability to sign their names.[245] Pierre could also read a bit, but only in French.

There were several members of the Cuevas and Ladner families living on Cat Island at various times during those early days. Since the population was sparse along the coast, it was not unusual that the children would become attracted to members of their own families. After all, these were the only people they were acquainted with for the most part. The early settlers often had no other choices. Others in the Cuevas and Ladner families had already intermarried, so it was not unusual when Perrique chose his cousin Marie Louise Ladner to be his wife. Since the couple were second cousins, it was necessary for them to receive a dispensation from the church before they could be married. Father Antonio de Sedella signed the following document:

> *On October 27, 1827, I, Antonio de Sedella, Religious Capuchin, Cure of the Church of St. Louis in New Orleans, having taken the necessary preparation and read the three Canonical banns during three solemn Masses and festive days, married and gave the nuptial blessing to Pedro Bautista Cuevas of the Lady of the Lake Parish in Ponchatoula, legitimate son of Juan Cuevas and of Maria Ladner, with Maria Louisa Ladner, native and resident of the same Parish, legitimate daughter of Juan Bautista Ladner and Francisca Fayard, giving them the dispensation for parental relationship. I received the mutual consent of both.*[246]

Marie was born on April 18, 1810, and was living with her parents on the north shore of Lake Ponchartrain at Ponchatoula. Perrique had moved to that area to find work. It was while he was there that he became attracted to Marie Louise Ladner, his second cousin, who was a year older than Perrique. She became pregnant, and on January 5, 1828, their first child, Pierre Simon, was born. They married in 1829, a year after their son's birth. After the wedding, Perrique and Marie first moved to a site on the Jordan River and then later to a home on Wolf River. A year later, their second child, Christopher, was born.

In October 1834, two years after the birth of their third child, Marie, Perrique purchased land from his cousin, Dominique Ladner. The land, situated on the north shore of Biloxi's Back Bay, was in the area now known as D'Iberville.[247] It was a beautiful lot with a 1,728-foot-long front on the water. From the bay on the north side, it stretched 6,720 feet to the north. The land to the east was owned by Emanuel Sanchez, and the land to the west was owned by his cousin Dominique.[248] Dominique was the son of Mathurin Ladner, one of the three sons of Christian Ladner.

On March 3, 1840, Perrique purchased a lot that was 60 feet wide by 116 feet deep on Lameuse Street in Biloxi from Eliza Ladner.[249] Eliza was the daughter of his cousin Jean Baptiste Ladner III. He built a general store on this lot, which he ran successfully for a number of years.

Pierre became a well-respected businessman in the village of Biloxi. His tall, dark good looks, combined with his outgoing, spontaneously warm-hearted personality, made him popular with his fellow shop owners as well as his customers. Everyone knew Perrique, but there was another name by which he was known. Behind his back, people were beginning to call him *macreau*; this is an old French term for what we call a "womanizer." Pierre had an eye for attractive ladies, and it was no secret.

One day in 1841, Marie Arsine Ladner, Perrique's second cousin, came into the store. She was distraught over the recent death of her husband, Victor LaForce. She seemed very fragile, and Perrique offered a sympathetic ear. Since she only lived a few doors down from the store, this distraught widow began to visit Perrique more often. What started as an innocent family tragedy quickly turned into something that neither had anticipated. Perrique fell madly in love with Arsine. The cousins became lovers, and before long, Arsine was pregnant with his child. To compound the situation, Perrique's wife, Marie Louise, was also Marie Arsine's cousin, creating a complicated incestuous family love triangle.

On March 18, 1841, Marie Louise, Perrique's wife, delivered a baby girl, Zoe, and that same year, on December 19, Marie Arsine, Perrique's lover, delivered their first child, Anatol Francois. At first, the affair had been kept secret, but with the birth of Arsine's baby, the secret became public knowledge. Needless to say, his wife, Louise, was shocked and hurt. A contrite Perrique expressed his sorrow and pledged his love, promising her that his affair with Arsine had ended. Louise accepted the apology, and soon, the couple's lives were back to a semblance of normalcy.

Francoise Emile, the seventh child of Perrique and Louise, was born on March 9, 1843. The family was so happy. It seemed that the affair with Arsine was long forgotten, but unbeknownst to Louise, Perrique and Arsine could not stay apart. They had continued to see each other on every occasion they could. The inevitable happened, and Arsine was again pregnant with a second child of Perrique's, whom they called Enos.

At first furious, Louise realized that Perrique and Arsine were not going to end their clandestine relationship. If she wanted to keep her family together, Louise had to turn a blind eye to Perrique's philandering. For reasons that are very difficult for most of us to understand, the two women accepted the arrangement and coexisted with Perrique as the head of their separate families. The community was shocked and dismayed as the two women continued to produce children almost simultaneously. In the end, Marie Louise, the wife, had a total of twelve children, while Marie Arsine had a total of seven, all by Perrique, *le macreau*. Perrique was the father of nineteen children, more than any other one of the Juan de Cuevas children.

In order to separate the families, Perrique purchased forty acres of land in Jackson County. This parcel is the western portion of what is now Gulf Hills. He left Biloxi and moved to this new home in 1847, six years after his affair with Arsine was made public.

Despite his weakness when it came to women, Pierre was a dedicated father. He had helped his oldest son, Pierre Simon, open a general store in their community on Back Bay. The store became an important part of the D'Iberville settlement. Along with the store, Pierre Simon also began operating a ferry across the bay, and he later opened a shipyard on the north shore.[250] The shipyard was described as being ninety-eight feet long on the bay, east by the "old ferry landing," and west by the home of his younger brother Christopher.

The Cuevas family became more upset with Perrique, as he continued to have children by both of his cousins. The business community was also angry that a prominent member of their city would openly flaunt such loose morals. The independent-minded Perrique paid no attention to their growing protests, although the pressure from both city officials and his family was growing. To make matters worse, Arsine was not only Perrique's cousin, but she was eight years older. Perrique's two families remained separated for obvious reasons and were never close. Many say that Perique's father, Juan, would have never tolerated such behavior from his arrogant son. Fortunately, Juan de Cuevas never knew of the situation, since he had died before the affair became public knowledge. Perrique's open disregard for morality and decency did, however, hurt his mother deeply. Alienated from the business community and his family, Perrique was finally forced to decide: would he leave his wife and his legitimate children, or would he do the right thing and give up his lover, Arsine?

In 1857, Perrique, Marie Arsine Ladner LaForce and their seven children left the Mississippi Gulf Coast forever and moved back to the north shore area of Lake Pontchartrain in St. Tammany Parrish, where he had originally met and married his only legitimate wife, their cousin, Marie Louise. Before he left, Perrique divided his estate on the coast equally among his twelve children. At that time, the Quave family owned most of the property on what is now Bay Shore Road. By 1928, however, the Quave family had settled mostly around Central Avenue in North Biloxi (now D'Iberville).[251] Perrique and Marie Louise Ladner remained married to each other for the rest of their lives, since both were devoutly Catholic, divorce was unacceptable. Arsine and Perrique, therefore, were never legally married.

Perrique was completely alienated from all but one of his legitimate children on the Gulf Coast. John Warne, who was only ten years old when Perrique left Biloxi, did remain close to his father. After John Warne married in 1865, he and his wife, Victoria Gollott, moved to Abita Springs so he could be near his father. At one point, according to Perrique's will, Perrique actually lived with John Warne. The devoted son took care of his aging father to the end. Perrique Cuevas died at his home in St. Tammany Parish at the age of eighty-one. Under Louisiana law, a man could only leave his estate to his legitimate children; therefore, Arsine's children received nothing from their father.

The drama in Perrique's family continued with the death of Victoria, John Warne's wife, in November 1887. Following in the reckless footsteps of his father, John Warne remarried on July 14, 1892. His new bride was Lorena Lavinghouse Penton, who was a full thirty years younger than John Warne. That in itself was not too strange because it was common for an older man to marry a very young wife—and remains so today. The twist in this story comes after John Warne's death on August 13, 1922. John Warne's widow, Lorena, married Peter H. Quave, John Warne's son by his first wife, Victoria Gollott. Louisiana law did not prohibit a man from marrying his stepmother.

Perrique's wife, Marie Louise Cuevas, lived in the Ocean Springs area until her death on May 18, 1888, at the age of eighty-seven. Perrique's children remained in the North Biloxi and North Ocean Springs area, and along with their families, they became a dominant force in local commerce. Perrique's son Pierre Simon was the most active of the children. With his father's help, Pierre Simon opened a mercantile store, a ferry service across Back Bay and, later, the Quave Shipyard.

Pierre Simon married Anna Mallet (Malley) in 1851. Shortly before the birth of their fourth child in 1863, Pierre Simon, along with his brother Christopher, enlisted in the Confederate army. Christopher was serving as the sheriff of Harrison County from 1856 until the two brothers joined the Live Oak Rifles at Ocean Springs. Some of his cousins had already been fighting in the Civil War, and in fact, Louis Henry Krohn had been killed. Unfortunately, neither Pierre Simon nor Christopher ever returned home. Both died while serving the South in the War Between the States.

Anna, Pierre Simon's widow, was left with a family of four very young children to care for. The oldest son, Ramon John Quave, who was only about ten years old when his father was killed, took over the role as head of the household. It was a tremendous burden for such a young boy, but he proved to be up to the task. He immediately began running his father's ferry business, transporting people and livestock back and forth across Back Bay. Jacquemine, a veteran boat builder, took him under his wing as an apprentice and taught him how to build boats. In 1888, when he was about thirty-five, Ramon went into the mercantile business with J.D. Mulholland. In a very short time, Ramon bought out Mr. Mulholland and continued to operate the store until his death in 1908. Ramon's daughter Madeleine became a well-known businesswoman in her own right. She started the Farmer's Cash Market in 1919 and built the Star Theater in 1921. She ran the Cash Market for decades until she retired in 1963. When Ramon died in 1908, he was described in his obituary as "the father of the village of Seymour."

The village on Back Bay was part of the unincorporated area of North Biloxi often referred to as Seymour. In 1927, a bridge called the D'Iberville Bridge was completed across the bay from Biloxi to Central Avenue.[252]

In September 1867, a few years after Pierre Simon's death, his widow, Anna, leased the Quave Shipyard to José Aval. The lease was for one hundred dollars per year for five years. After that lease was up, the shipyard was leased to Pedro Perez, a Spanish immigrant and ship carpenter. The shipyard continued to function into the 1890s, run by Peter (Pierre II), Ramon's brother. After the shipyard was closed, Peter started a seafood business. The business was called the Peter Quave Packing Company and was located on Central Avenue in D'Iberville on the current site of C.F. Gollotte & Son Seafood Inc.[253] The people who used the ferry to travel to and from Biloxi could stop and water their horses there. Peter kept a cement tub in front of his seafood factory, where fresh water was always flowing.

Peter died in 1936, and like his brother Ramon, he was also connected to the development of North Biloxi. In the book *Twentieth Century Coast Edition of the* Biloxi Daily Herald, which was published in 1902, Peter Quave is described as being "among the solid and respected men of the community… working for the betterment and advancement of this section of the country." The descendants of Peter Quave have been merchants at Back Bay, operating stores near the bay front for almost one hundred years.

Ursin, one of Perrique's sons, received land from his father, when he disposed of his holdings on the coast. In 1870, Ursin and his wife, Mamie Sarah Davis, donated some of this land for the establishment of the Antioch Baptist Church.[254] A cemetery for the burial of Quave family members was later created on a portion of this 185-acre parcel.[255] This was quite appropriate since his father, Perrique, had owned the land for many years.[256] Ursin also served with the Live Oak Rifles, Company "A," Third Infantry

Regiment of the Third Brigade Army of Mississippi. While Ursin did survive the Civil War, his son Christopher, along with Perrique's son Pierre Simon, were killed in action.

Perrique's son Joseph first married Nancy Entrekin, with whom he had nine children. After her death on November 11, 1907, he married Della Hardy Rosetti. Joseph and Della had only one son, Lazrus "Laz" Quave. Laz, Perrique's grandson, became one of the most popular and visible members of the Quave family. Laz served as deputy sheriff, sheriff, a member of the board of supervisors, mayor of Biloxi and as a councilman of the City of Biloxi.

Laz had eight children. His son Russell retired in 1992 as vice-president of the Peoples Bank of Biloxi, and he was the first branch manager and loan officer of the D'Iberville–St. Martin Branch, where he was employed for 20 years. Prior to joining the bank, he was the manager of the Goodyear Tire and Rubber Company of Biloxi from 1955 through the 1960s. He was recognized as a hometown banker who laid the groundwork for D'Iberville to become a city, and he devoted countless hours to Catholic causes. His proudest moment came when his son Russell "Rusty" Quave was elected mayor of the City of D'Iberville, a position he still currently holds (in 2020). In addition to being mayor, Rusty continues to operate his meat market and convenience store on the same road, now called Central Avenue, on which his Quave ancestors had labored over 150 years ago.

Perrique left the largest legacy on the coast of any of the other children of Juan de Cuevas, his scandalous life and his banishment from the Biloxi area notwithstanding. Pierre died in 1889 at Abita Springs in St. Tammany Parish. He was buried in Covington, Louisiana.

Charles Ferdinand Cuevas

Charles Ferdinand Cuevas was born in 1811 on Cat Island. Charles and Perrique were the only two of the Cuevas children who learned to write their names, although they had no formal education. Charles was gentle, even-tempered, good-natured and slow to anger. This made him a very solid husband and father.

In 1834, Charles married Rose Desiree Caillavet, the daughter of Louis Caillavet and Marguerite Fayard of Biloxi. The couple had nine children: Rose Emma, Adeline, Caroline, Louise, Louis, Maria, Sophia, Laurent and Charles. Rose Desiree's nephew Raymond "Medeaux" Caillavet served as mayor of Biloxi from 1877 to 1882. Rose Desiree's father, Louis Caillavet, had arrived in Biloxi from the Opelousas Post in Louisiana around 1810. He was fluent in both French and English and often served his neighbors as an interpreter and counsel in legal matters. At times, he was the only person in Biloxi who could read and write.[257] It is from Charles Caillavet that the Cuevas boys, Charles and Perrique, learned to read and write on a limited basis. Charles was very industrious and worked very hard—he was not afraid of getting his hands dirty. He and Rose spent their entire lives in the Biloxi area. They lived next door to the Caillavets on Cuevas street, a street named after Charles.[258] Charles and Rose were well liked and respected in Biloxi.

Rose died in 1883 at the age of sixty-nine, leaving Charles to live alone for the remainder of his life. He died eleven years later, in 1894. Both Charles and Rose were buried in a tomb in the Old Biloxi Cemetery, a short distance behind the tomb of his parents, Juan de Cuevas and Marie Ladner.

Ramon Cuevas

Ramon was born on Cat Island in 1812. He was the youngest son of Juan and Marie. Being the baby boy, he was spoiled by his older sisters. This may account for his fastidious nature. Family stories suggest that his heightened sense of hygiene and cleanliness were faults that made him a poor farmer. He did not like working in the dirt. Ramon, who had a very technical mind, was particularly interested in the lighthouse that the United States government had begun building on the western tip of Cat Island. Had he lived in a later time, Ramon may well have been an engineer, but for a young man without any hope of obtaining a formal education, this lighthouse was fascinating. Since the lighthouse was only about two miles from the Cuevas home, Ramon spent as much time on the site as possible, watching the construction.

Mr. George Riolly of Pass Christian had been chosen as the first lighthouse keeper and was in charge of overseeing the work. Ramon and George spent a lot of time together, and when Mr. Riolly's wife, Isabelle, later joined her husband on the island, the three of them became close friends.

The lighthouse was formally completed on June 10, 1831, but its operation was not actually begun for several months, due to a shortage of whale oil fuel to power the light. Unfortunately, just a short time after it opened, George Riolly became ill with smallpox. Since Ramon had been actively involved with the lighthouse from the beginning, he was familiar with all of the duties. He quickly pitched in to help Isabelle maintain the lighthouse schedule.

The disease took its toll, and George did not survive. Since Ramon never liked farming, working at the lighthouse offered him the perfect opportunity to do something he had truly grown to love. He immediately applied with the government to fill the vacant position. He was easily confirmed as the obvious choice to become the second lighthouse keeper on Cat Island.

With her husband then deceased, Isabelle had no place to go. The house where she and George had been living had been built next to the lighthouse by the government for the keeper and their family. Ramon allowed her to continue living there since he could stay with his family down the beach. It wasn't long, however, before the close friendship between Ramon and Isabelle developed into something more. To no one's surprise, he moved into the house with Isabelle. They were both only twenty-two years old, and it was understandable how a romance between these young people could develop. On April 4, 1834, they were married in New Orleans—but not before Isabelle had become pregnant with their first child.[259] Their daughter Isabelle Euphrosine was born in that same year. Ramon and Isabelle had three more children—all born on Cat Island.

One gloomy Monday morning in 1849, on the twenty-fourth day of September, Ramon received the sad news that his father, Juan, had been found dead. Ramon took the news of his father's death very hard. But no one was prepared for the tragedy that was about to occur. In the midst of mourning for his father, his wife, Isabelle, also died. Her untimely death occurred on Wednesday, September 26, just two days after Juan de Cuevas had died.

Ramon was left to raise his four young children. Euphrosine, the oldest, was fifteen, and Charles Oscar, the youngest, was six when their mother died. He was fully aware that he could not raise the children by himself. They needed a woman's guidance. It wasn't long before he met the lovely Irma Monet.

Ramon was well known in the local community, and as the lighthouse keeper, he became very active in community affairs. His position brought him into contact with Mr. Julius Caesar Monet, a prominent attorney of the time. Through Mr. Monet, Ramon met his young daughter Irma. Irma had, herself, been recently widowed. She had been living in New Orleans with her husband, a Mr. Wilkinson, who was a banker in the city. The couple had two sons who apparently died at the same time as her husband, either by accident or by disease. After they were buried in New Orleans, she returned to Bay St. Louis to be with her family.

The young widow was instantly attracted to the tall young lighthouse keeper and made every effort to be in his company. Her attention did not go unnoticed. Ramon fell madly in love with this young girl. After a very short courtship, he proposed, and on a beautiful Sunday afternoon in the city of New Orleans, they were married. Ramon married Desiree "Irma" Monet Wilkinson on November 3, 1850.

Less than two years later, Ramon and Irma had their first child. Marie Alphonsine was born in December 1852. The children from his first marriage were crazy about their new sister. The boys started calling her "Tootie," a name that stayed with her throughout her entire life. The couple had three more children, Robert Joseph, Cornelia Celeste and Agnes Gabrielle, before the family left Cat Island.

In 1861, a series of three severe hurricanes devastated the coast, including Cat Island. Ramon and his family evacuated just as the last of the three storms swept through their home. The lighthouse, which had been built on the sand with little regard to a strong foundation, was virtually destroyed. No longer functional, the government closed the lighthouse in July of that year. With the closing of the lighthouse, Ramon and his family moved to Shieldsborough (now Bay St. Louis) to start a new life.

With word that the lighthouse had been closed and that the family had left Cat Island, Ramon's sons by Isabelle decided to join the army to fight with the South in the War Between the States. On June 29, 1861, Ramon Jr., James and Charles were formally enrolled into service at Shieldsborough as members of the Shieldsborough Rifles, Third Mississippi Infantry, CSA.

Ramon's son James became one of the most popular veterans living at Beauvoir, then a last home for Confederate veterans and their wives. He became known as the "Sage of Beauvoir" because of his keen wit and warm personality. He is the source for much of the information about Cat Island and the original Cuevas family.

The late congressman Hale Boggs (1914–1972) of Louisiana was Ramon's great-great-grandson. Ramon's daughter Agnes Gabrielle married Thomas Hale in 1879. Their daughter Josephine Claire Hale married William Boggs on March 7, 1909. William's father, Robert, was an artist and writer from Georgia who moved to the coast in 1875 with his wife, Liza Jane. He purchased seven acres of beachfront land in what is now Long Beach. They built their home there and called it Breezydale. On the death of their son, William inherited the property, and he and his wife, Josephine Claire, moved into the house and raised five children there. Their oldest son, Thomas Hale Boggs, became famous as the Democratic whip in the U.S. Congress and, later, the Democratic majority leader. He died in an airplane crash in 1972. Unfortunately, a hurricane destroyed Breezydale, but the Boggs family who inherited the property rebuilt and continued to live there. The property and the eleven houses that were eventually built there became known as Boggsdale. Boggsdale was a legendary location in Mississippi Coast history that was totally destroyed by Hurricane Katrina in 2005.

Ramon died unexpectedly at the age of fifty-seven, shortly after moving to Shieldsborough. He was buried in an unmarked grave in Cedar Rest Cemetery at Bay St. Louis. Later, when Ramon's son James died, he was buried next to his father.

Ramon's wife, Irma, died on January 6, 1910, at the age of eighty-nine, while living with her granddaughter Irma Hale in Gulfport. She was buried in St. Mary's Cemetery at Bay St. Louis. Her headstone reads, simply, "Irma Cuevas, 1820–1910."[260]

Euphrosine Cuevas

Euphrosine Cuevas was born on July 18, 1813, on Cat Island. She was the most reserved and, some would say, withdrawn of all of the Cuevas children. She tended to be emotional and would often overact. Her tendency to be withdrawn is evident in the fact that very little is really known about her or her children. She married Pierre Nolasque Guardia when she was thirty.[261] That was relatively old for a young lady to marry in the 1800s. This was partially because of her shy and moody personality. Apparently, her husband shared many of those negative traits.

Pierre was the son of Raphael Guardia and Paula Marti. By some accounts, Raphael was a doctor, but little is definitely known about Pierre or his parents. Even before their official wedding, Euphrosine and Pierre had defied their families' wishes and had moved to a site on the Jordan River. They set up a house without the benefit of marriage, which distressed the devoutly Catholic Cuevas family. Their first child, Raphael Guardia, was born in 1839, and their second child, Pierre Guardia II, came two years later. Finally giving into pressure, the couple was married on September 3, 1843. Because of their minimal contact with others along the coast, they seldom ever saw the visiting priests. When the wedding was finally scheduled, it was arranged for the priest to also baptize their two sons. In a double ceremony, the parents were first married, and then the children were baptized afterward.[262]

It would be four years before Euphrosine and Pierre had their next child, Paula. The couple eventually had eight children. The youngest, Timothy Peter, was born in 1845.[263]

No further records of this family have been found. No one knows when Euphrosine or Pierre Guardia died, but they were buried together in the Rotten Bayou Cemetery. And while we do have the birth records of the children, no one knows when or where any of them died.

Henriette Pauline Cuevas

Henriette Pauline was the last child born to Juan de Cuevas and his wife, Marie. The little girl was born on a blustery Thursday, the second day of February 1815, less than a year after the Battle of New Orleans. She was very intelligent and was always clear and concise in her thinking. In spite of her magnetic and outgoing personality, she did not make friends easily. This was possibly due to her dogmatic opinions. Unfortunately, there have been many in the Cuevas family who have shared this fault.

When she was twenty-one years old and still living with her family, a young Spanish immigrant, José Vasquez, visited the Moran family, who was also living on the island. José came to America from the Galicia Province in the northwest part of Spain in the 1830s. His parents, Bernardo Vasquez and Theresa LaCruz, like so many other families in Spain, never saw or heard from their children again after they left for the Louisiana colonies. Such a permanent separation was indicative of the strong commitment these new arrivals made to their new families and their newly chosen homes.

After only one visit, José made every excuse he could find to return to the island to see Henrietta. Over time, the relationship grew, and in 1837, they were married. Like many of the Cuevas children and some of the grandchildren, the newly married couple made their first home on the Cuevas family's island. François, the first child born to Henriette and José, came nine months after the couple was married.

In 1840, José purchased property on Old Fort Bayou, northeast of the settlement called East Biloxi. Fourteen years later, the area became known as Ocean Springs. The Vasquez family moved from Cat Island to their new home that same year; there, José made his living first as a sailor and later as a baker. In the late 1850s, he opened an account in Pierre Quave's store on Back Bay in North Biloxi.[264] Over time, José purchased more property in that section.

In 1841, the year after they moved from Cat Island, the couple's second child, Josephine, was born. José and Henrietta had ten children. The other eight children were: François (1838–?), Josephine (1840–1881), Joseph

(1841–1935), Theresa (1843–1910), Harriet (Henrietta, 1847–1875), Caroline (1848–1924), Mary (1852–1917), Bernard (1854–1920), Seymore (1855–?) and Pauline (1859–1946).[265]

We do not know when José died, but on June 2, 1879, his estate was divided between his children. His son Bernard inherited property on which the old Basque (Vasquez) Cemetery is located. Bernard's inheritance excluded the 150 square feet that was reserved for the family graveyard.[266] Henrietta died on September 22, 1856. She and José were both buried in the old Basque (Vasquez) Cemetery, near Bayou Porto in Jackson County, along with other members of their family.

NOTES

Introduction

1. Cassibry, *Ladner Odyssey*, 66.
2. Ephraim Kirby (1757–1804), the special commissioner on the Spanish boundary under President Thomas Jefferson, sent a census report to President Thomas Jefferson on May 1, 1804.
3. Cassibry, *Ladner Odyssey*, 112.

1. Cemeteries in America

4. Cothran and Danylchak, *Grave Landscapes*, 144–45.
5. Darity, "Burial Grounds," 392–93.
6. Etlin, "Père Lachaise," 211–22.
7. Bunting and Nylander, *Old Cambridge*, 69.
8. Williams, "In the Garden Cemetery."
9. Cothran and Danylchak, *Grave Landscapes*, 36.
10. Chen, "Free Time with Dead People."
11. Schexnayder and Manhein, *Fragile Grounds*, 24.

2. *The Old Biloxi Cemetery*

12. Harrison County Deed Book 3, 36–37.
13. Cassibry, *Ladner Odyssey*, 121.
14. O'Neill and Giraud, "French Louisiana," 303–6.
15. Lossky, *Political Power*, 110.
16. Margry, *Découvertes*, 31–142.
17. "Historical French Documents," Parke-Bernet Galleries.
18. McWilliams, *Fleur de Lys*, 58.
19. Murphy, *John Law*, 335–39.
20. Hough, *Mississippi Bubble*, 142.
21. Gayarré, *History of Louisiana*, 101.
22. Ibid., 168.
23. Ibid., 231.
24. Phelps, *Louisiana*, 63.
25. According to the 1810 U.S. Census, New Orleans had a population of ten thousand, making it the fifth-largest American city after New York, Philadelphia, Boston and Baltimore. In the next thirty years, New Orleans grew faster than any other American city, so that by the 1830 census, it had become the third-largest American city behind New York and Baltimore.
26. Kelley, "Yellow Fever."

3. *Noteworthy in the Old Biloxi Cemetery*

27. Find A Grave, "Edward Charles Barq, Sr.," www.findagrave.com.
28. FamilySearch, "Louisiana, Parish Marriages."
29. Eric's Gourmet Root Beer Site, "History of Root Beer."
30. Bottle Books, "Digging."
31. Eric's Gourmet Root Beer Site, "History of Root Beer."
32. BevReview, "Barq's."
33. Levy, "Sarsaparilla."
34. Over Caffeinated, "Barq's Root Beer."
35. Coca-Cola, "Barq's."
36. U.S. Army Center of Military History, "Special Unit Designations."
37. United States Geological Survey, "Black Hills."
38. Robinson, *Diaries*, 247.
39. U.S. Statute 19, 254. Enacted on February 28, 1877.
40. United States Army Center of Military History, "Indian Wars."

41. Cassibry, *Early Settlers*, 24, 50, 118–19.
42. Jackson County, Mississippi Land Deed Book, 96, 325–26.
43. Rowland and Howell, *Military History*, 137.
44. Lepre, *Caillavet Family*, 30, 66, 76.
45. Lepre, *Catholic Church Records*, 45–48.
46. Harrison County, Mississippi Land Deed Book, 15, 24–25.
47. *Pascagoula Democrat-Star*, January 9, 1885, 2.
48. *Pascagoula Democrat-Star*, October 5, 1883, 3.
49. Sigma Chi Fraternity, "Founding."
50. Harding, *Literary Societies*, 79.
51. Riccards, "Whitelaw."
52. Runkle, *Sigma Chi Quarterly*, 323–25.
53. Ibid.
54. Beta Theta Pi, *The Beta Theta Pi*, 61–62.
55. Sigma Chi Fraternity, "History."
56. Runkle, *Sigma Chi Quarterly*, 323–25.
57. Cathedral of the Immaculate Conception, Mobile, baptism book 2, 69.
58. Crump, "Tortured Cat Islander."
59. Juan's size is based on the average height of his family, who I met during a recent visit to Algámitas, Spain.
60. Obituary, *Daily Picayune*.
61. Visit to the house by the author on September 13, 2007.
62. On April 30, 1791, the governor of Louisiana Estéban Rodriguez Miró y Sabater Miró issued orders for a census. The only people listed at that time on Cat Island were Nicholas Christian; his wife and ten children; José Morin and his wife, Marie Louise; Nicholas's daughter; two free Black men, José Klucer and José Mirer; and a free mulatto named Diequir Duret. In that census, Juan de Cuevas was not mentioned anywhere on the coast.
63. Chatterton, *Cutters and Smugglers*.
64. Index cards, Louisiana State Museum Library.
65. Martin, *History of Louisiana*, 325.
66. Pintado Papers.
67. Bremer, "Amichel."
68. Ibid.
69. There is no marriage record for Juan and Marie, but based on the existing baptismal records of some of their children and a Spanish permit dated September 10, 1795, it is certain they were married sometime in 1795.
70. Pintado Papers.
71. *Newsletter of the Florida Energy Extension Service* (March 1991).

72. Cassibry, *Early Settlers*, 137–38.
73. Deed dated July 24, 1810.
74. Jefferson, *Works*, 67–68.
75. Sullivan and Powell, *Gulf Coast*, 34, 35.
76. Juan de Cuevas was not directly involved with the Battle of New Orleans, and he did not take information to General Jackson. This is a story that has been mistakenly passed down for generations. For the full explanation of how the legend began, see my book *Cat Island: The History of a Mississippi Gulf Coast Barrier Island* (North Carolina: McFarland & Company Inc., 2011), 97–105.
77. The legend of Juan de Cuevas as a hero in the Battle of New Orleans is folklore. Juan de Cuevas was termed the "Hero of Cat Island" after he captured two pirates in the gulf off the island coast. For this brave deed, he was given a cash award by the state. The story of this heroic action has become mixed with his supposed involvement in the War of 1812. (See site 7, Juan de Cuevas Captures the Pirate.)
78. Facts are confirmed by the state document, "An Act for the Relief of John Quavre," *Journal in the House of Representative of the Fifth Session of the General Assembly*, State of Mississippi, signed by Cawles Mead, speaker of the house of representatives, and James Pattan, lieutenant governor and president of the senate (November 24, 1821).
79. Morrison, *Funeral Customs*, 77–80.
80. Ibid.
81. Ibid., 26.
82. Mayer, *Embalming*, 69–74.
83. Posey, "Gulf Coast Reminiscences," 4.
84. Warner, *Generals in Gray*, 68–69.
85. Wheeler et al., *Confederate Military*, 249–50.
86. Ibid.
87. Godspeed Brothers, *Memoirs of Mississippi*, 67.
88. *Biloxi Daily Herald*, "Davis."
89. Lever, *Marie Antoinette*, 63–65.
90. Lepre, *Delaunay Family*, 19–21.
91. Ibid., 25.
92. Cassibry, *Ladner Odyssey*, 693.
93. Lepre, *Delaunay*, 31–33.
94. Boudreaux, *Seafood Capital*, 37.
95. 1880 Harrison Co., Mississippi federal census, T9_648, 8, ED 139.
96. *Pascagoula Democrat-Star*, December 30, 1881, 3.

97. *Biloxi Daily Herald*, October 13, 1894, 8.
98. *Biloxi Daily Herald*, October 20, 1894, 8, 10; *Biloxi Daily Herald*, November 1894, 8, 15; *Biloxi Daily Herald*, December 1894, 7; *Biloxi Daily Herald*, March 9, 1895, 8.
99. *Biloxi Daily Herald* (Twentieth Century Coast Edition), 1902, 20.
100. *Daily Herald*, December 6, 1922, 3; *Daily Herald*, December 28, 1923; *Daily Herald*, February 27, 1923, 3; *Daily Herald*, July 10, 1923, 3.
101. *Biloxi Daily Herald*, September 19, 1903, 8.
102. *Biloxi Daily Herald*, September 7, 1898, 4.
103. Lang, *Harrison County*, 97–99.
104. *Biloxi Daily Herald*, March 19, 1892, 4.
105. *Biloxi Daily Herald*, October 20, 1904, 5.
106. *Biloxi Daily Herald*, January 21, 1905, 5.
107. Perez, "Infamous Hermit."
108. The story as told by E.W. Suarez, a research assistant of the Biloxi Local History and Genealogy Department.
109. Eastern State Penitentiary, "Home."
110. Kahan, *Eastern State Penitentiary*, 67.
111. Johnston, *Eastern State Penitentiary*, 37.
112. National Park Service, "Eastern State Penitentiary," National Historic Landmark Summary Listing, www.nps.gov, June 6, 2008.
113. Perez, "Hermit of Deer Island."
114. *Daily Herald*, May 28, 1959.
115. Powell, *"Skeet,"* 52.
116. Hardy, "Boeuf Gras."
117. Powell, *"Skeet,"* 64.
118. Beaugez, "Sunken Resort."
119. Find A Grave, "Memorial # 39730635," www.findagrave.com.
120. *Daily Herald*, October 30, 1931, 6.
121. *Daily Herald*, May 29, 1938, 5.
122. Ibid.
123. Find A Grave, "Memorial # 39730635."
124. Boudreaux, *Seafood Capital*, 47.
125. *Biloxi Daily Herald*, September 26, 1903, 1.
126. Harrison Co., Mississippi, Marriage Record Book 6, 76.
127. Nuwer, "Biloxi Fishermen."
128. *Baltimore Sun*, January 13, 1922.
129. "Biloxi Chief Industry," *Biloxi Daily Herald*, September 12, 1892, 4.
130. *Biloxi Daily Herald*, December 21, 1889, 4.

131. *Biloxi Daily Herald*, January 21, 1893, 4.
132. *Biloxi Daily Herald*, February 25, 1893, 8.
133. Cramer, "White Pillars."
134. *Daily Herald*, September 26, 1902.
135. *Biloxi Daily Herald*, October 19, 1903, 1.
136. Ibid.
137. Murphy, Melton and Ward, *African American Religions*, 158.
138. Josephites, "Our Mission."
139. Ibid.
140. Murphy, Melton and Ward, *African American Religions*, 159.
141. Martin, "Eugene Marino."
142. Ibid.
143. Find A Grave, "Eugene Antonio Marino," www.findagrave.com.
144. "Eugene Marino," obituary, *New York Times*, November 16, 2000.
145. ArtCyclopedia, "George E. Ohr Art Links," www.artcyclopedia.com, January 22, 2008.
146. "George Ohr Teapot," *Antiques and the Arts Weekly*.
147. Collectics, "Ohr Pottery."
148. Albertson, "Odyssey."
149. *Daily Herald*, March 17, 1930, 10.
150. "Rago, David (appraiser, Dallas, Texas)," *Antiques Roadshow*.
151. The Attic, "Mad Potter."
152. AskArt, "George Edgar b. Ohr, (1857–1918)," www.askart.com.
153. *SunHerald*, March 4, 1997, C-2.
154. Manning, *Air Education*.
155. Find A Grave, "Anthony V. Ragusin (22 Apr 1902–3 Mar 1997)," www.findagrave.com.
156. National Park Service, "NPS Focus."
157. Mississippi Gulf Coast Convention and Visitors Bureau.
158. Ownby, Wilson and Harris, "Pleasant Reed House," 169.
159. Ohr-O'Keefe Museum of Art, "Pleasant Reed Interpretive Center."
160. Ibid.
161. *Daily Herald*, April 9, 1942, 1, 6.
162. *Daily Herald*, September 7, 1934, 1, 4.
163. Dyer, *Along the Gulf*.
164. *Daily Herald*, April 9, 1942, 1, 6.
165. Ibid.
166. *Daily Herald*, September 7, 1934, 1, 4.
167. Ibid.

168. United States Coast Guard, "Lighthouses."
169. U.S. Coast Guard Historian's Office, U.S. Coast Guard Headquarters, 2100 Second Street Southwest, Washington, D.C., 20593-0001.
170. Lepre, *Seymour Family*, 41.
171. U.S. Census Bureau, "U.S. Census, 1850."
172. American State Papers, 1994.
173. Jackson County, Mississippi Land Deed Book, 87, 491–92.
174. Jackson County, Mississippi Land Deed Book, 185, 357–59.

4. The Tomb Boom

175. Advertisement, *Southern Galaxy*, March 11, 1830, 4.
176. Pearce and Giraud, *History of French Louisiana*, 248–49.
177. *New Orleans Crescent*, July 27, 1850, 2.

5. Secrets of the Cuevas Tomb

178. Posey, "Gulf Coast Reminiscences," 4.
179. Schexnayder and Manhein, *Fragile Grounds*, 67.

6. The Mystery Woman

180. *Daily Herald*, January 25, 1890, 3.
181. *Daily Herald*, August 30, 1918, 6.
182. *Daily Herald*, September 21, 1898, 11.
183. Bradford O'Keefe Funeral Records, book 2, 181.
184. *Daily Herald*, November 7, 1921, 3.
185. *Daily Herald*, August 30, 1918, 5.
186. *Daily Herald*, May 6, 1935, 2.

Appendix

187. Malcom Daniel, "Daguerre (1787–1851) and the Invention of Photography," Metropolitan Museum of Art, October 2004, www.metmuseum.org.

188. Pollack, *Picture History*, 50.
189. Ibid.
190. Bible, James 4:14.
191. Headstone, Old Biloxi Cemetery; Cassibry, *Ladner Odyssey*, 711.
192. Bremer, "Amichel."
193. "It is agreed, that...the confines between the dominions of his Britannick Majesty and those of his Most Christian Majesty, in that part of the world, shall be fixed irrevocably by a line drawn along the middle of the River Mississippi, from its source to the river Iberville, and from hence, by a line drawn along the middle of this river, and the lakes Maurepas and Ponchartrain to the sea; and for this purpose, the Most Christian King cedes in full right, and guaranties to his Britannick Majesty, the river, and port of Mobile, and everything which he possesses, or ought to possess, on the left side of the river Mississippi, except the town of New Orleans and the island in which it is situated, which shall remain to France." (Article VII of the Treaty of Paris [1973] at Wikisource).
194. Bremer, "Amichel."
195. Rowland, *Register of the State*, 285–90.
196. Pintado Papers.
197. F. Martin, *History of Louisiana*, 325.
198. Bremer, "Amichel."
199. Headstone, Old Biloxi Cemetery; Cassibry, *Ladner Odyssey*, 711.
200. Pintado Papers.
201. There is some question as to when Nicholas Ladner died. No records have been found to verify a date. Some historians believe he died before moving to "Old Chimneys." The fact that his widow was eventually granted this land seems to indicate that his death occurred prior to actually taking possession of the land.
202. Confirmed by the subsequent survey of the Barhelemy Pellerin Land Grant of 1809 (Cassibry, *Ladner Odyssey*).
203. Inscription on the tomb of Juan and Marie de Cuevas in the Old Biloxi Cemetery.
204. Morrison, *Funeral Customs*, 101.
205. St. Louis Cathedral, New Orleans, Louisiana, marriage book 3 (1806–1821), 2,246 A 818.
206. Posey, "Gulf Coast Reminiscences," 2–3.
207. Cathedral of the Immaculate Conception, Mobile, baptism book 2, 92A.
208. St. Louis Cathedral, baptism book 9 (1818–1822).

209. Harrison County Census 1850.
210. Ibid.
211. Harrison County Census 1860, 1870, 1880.
212. Cathedral of the Immaculate Conception, Mobile, baptism book 2, 69.
213. St. Louis Cathedral, New Orleans, Louisiana, marriage book 3 (1806–1821), 238 A 948.
214. Cathedral of the Immaculate Conception, Mobile, baptism book 2, 69.
215. Hancock County Deed Book D, 173–74.
216. Hancock County Deed Book E, 674.
217. Ibid., 51.
218. Cassibry, *Ladner Odyssey*, 50.
219. Our Lady of the Gulf, marriage book 1, 8 A 35; 16 A 61; 6 A 29.
220. Headstone in Rotten Bayou Cemetery.
221. Hancock County Deed Book, 1893, 399.
222. Ibid.
223. St. Louis Cathedral, New Orleans, Louisiana, marriage book 3 (1806–1821), 238 A 948.
224. Deed Books 1 and 2, Harrison County Office of Chancery Clerk at the Courthouse in Gulfport, Mississippi.
225. St. Louis Cathedral, New Orleans, Louisiana baptism book 11 (1825–1827), 100 A 356.
226. Harrison County, marriage book 3, 15; Harrison County Census 1860.
227. An article by Julia Guice and Nap Cassibry published by the Mississippi Coast Historical and Genealogy Society.
228. St. Louis Cathedral, baptism book 2, 78a.
229. Cathedral of the Immaculate Conception, baptism book 2, 96.
230. My grandmother "Aunt Katrine" (Catherine Garriga Cuevas) was Ramon's daughter. She is my source for much of the family's information.
231. St. Louis Cathedral, marriage book 4 (1821–1830), 74 A 372.
232. Harrison County Deed Book 6, 513–14.
233. Harrison County Deed Book 6, 515–16
234. Cathedral of the Immaculate Conception, baptism book 2, 109.
235. Cassibry, *Ladner Odyssey*, 730.
236. Certificate of marriage, November 16, 1829, between Marie Solitelle Cuevas and Henry Auguste Krohn. (Archives of the Archdiocese of New Orleans, vol. 4, 174, act. no. 693.)
237. Harrison County Deed Book 5, 385–86.
238. From the Jean Baptiste Carco claim.
239. Harrison County Deed Book 1, 167–68.

240. Harrison County Deed Book 3, 73.
241. Lepre, *Krohn Family*, 47–50.
242. Harrison County Deed Book 7, 8.
243. Harrison County Deed Book 9, 436–37.
244. St. Louis Cathedral, marriage book 4, 106 A 483.
245. The signatures of Pierre and Charles appear on the document that was used to free Juan and Marie's enslaved people after the deaths of his parents.
246. St. Louis Cathedral, marriage book 4, 106 A 483.
247. Harrison County Deed Book 2, 193–94.
248. From Harrison County lawsuit *Laroissini v. Heirs of Carco*, April 11, 1852. Sworn statement by Pierre Cuevas.
249. Harrison County Deed Book 2, 95–197.
250. Pierre Quave Store Journal (1857–1862), from the archives of the Biloxi Public Library.
251. Ray Bellande, Land Map 1928, D'Iberville.
252. Ellis, *Mississippi Gulf Coast*, 39.
253. Harrison County Deed Book 10, 450.
254. Jackson County Deed Book 5, 443.
255. Harrison County Deed Book 9, 257–58.
256. Jackson County Deed Book 32, 311.
257. Cassibry, *Early Settlers*, 37.
258. Harrison County Deed Book 15, 24–25.
259. St. Louis Cathedral, marriage book 5 (1830–1834) A, 440.
260. Cassibry, *Ladner Odyssey*, 763.
261. St. Louis Cathedral, marriage book 8 (1840–1842) A, 106.
262. St. Louis Cathedral, baptism book 18 (1842), 21 A, 68.
263. Ibid.
264. Pierre Quave Store Journal (1857–1862), from the archives of the Biloxi Public Library.
265. Cassibry, *Ladner Odyssey*, 732, 773–74.
266. Jackson County Deed Book 4, 234–36.

BIBLIOGRAPHY

Albertson, Karla Klein. "The Odyssey of George E. Ohr." *Antiques and the Arts*, September 2, 2003.

Alexander, Mary Ellen. *Rosalie and Radishes: A History of Long Beach, Mississippi.* Gulfport, MS: Dixie Press, 1980.

American State Papers, 1994.

Antiques and the Arts Weekly. "Record George Ohr Teapot Leads Craftsman Auction." February 11, 2003.

The Attic. "The Mad Potter of Biloxi." www.theattic.space.

Baltimore Sun, January 13, 1922.

Beaugez, Jim. "Sunken Resort Island to Resurface for Biloxi Exhibit." *Clarion-Ledger*, June 10, 2016.

Beta Theta Pi. *The Beta Theta Pi* 13 (1885): 61–62.

BevReview. "Review: Barq's Red Crème Soda." www.bevreview.com.

Biloxi Daily Herald. "Gen. Joseph R. Davis." September 19, 1896.

Biloxi Daily Herald, 1889–1959.

Bottle Books. "Digging for Facts." www.bottlebooks.com.

Boudreaux, Edmond. *The Seafood Capital of the World: Biloxi's Maritime History*. Charleston, SC: The History Press, 2011.

Bradford O'Keefe Funeral Records. Book 2.

Bremer, Laville. "Amichel, A Narrative History of the Gulf Coast." *Times-Picayune*, January 2, 1944.

Bunting, Bainbridge, and Robert H. Nylander. *Old Cambridge*. Cambridge, MA: Cambridge Historical Commission, 1973.

Cassibry, Nap L., II. *Early Coast Families: The Ladner Odyssey*. Biloxi: Mississippi Gulf Coast Historical and Genealogical Society, 1987.

———. *Early Settlers and Land Grants at Biloxi*. Vol. 2. Biloxi: Mississippi Coast History and Genealogical Society, 1986.

Cathedral of the Immaculate Conception, Mobile. Baptism Book 2, 69.

Chatterton, E. Keble. *King's Cutters and Smugglers: 1700–1855*. Charleston, SC: BiblioBazaar, June 12, 2007.

Chen, Adrian. "I Spend My Free Time with Dead People—The Strange Hobby of Graving." www.slate.com.

Coca-Cola. "Coca-Cola Brand Fact Sheets—Barq's." www.coca-cola.com.

Collectics. "George E. Ohr Pottery & Ceramics Information & History." Collectors Reference and Collector Education. www.collectics.com.

Cothran, James R., and Erica Danylchak, *Grave Landscapes: The Nineteenth-Century Rural Cemetery Movement*. Columbia: University of South Carolina, 2018.

Cramer, Marguerite Scholtes. "White Pillars." *Down South Magazine*, September–October 1970.

Crump, Nannie Mayes. "Tortured Cat Islander Helped Save City from British, Says Grandson," *Times-Picayune*, Sunday, January 10, 1937.

Daily Delta, July 27, 1850.

Daily Picayune. Obituary. September 27, 1849. (It appeared in three languages, English, French and Spanish.)

Darity, William A., Jr. "Burial Grounds." *International Encyclopedia of the Social Sciences*. 2nd ed. Vol. 1. Detroit, MI: Macmillan Reference U.S., 2008.

Dyer, Charles Lawrence. *Along the Gulf: An Entertaining Story of an Outing Among the Beautiful Resorts on the Mississippi Sound from New Orleans, La., to Mobile, Ala., Being a Complete Description of the Advantages Which May Be Enjoyed During a Vacation Spent Among the Delightful Seaside Towns of the Mexican Gulf; Together with a Detailed Account of the Thriving Mississippi Cities of Waveland, Mississippi City, Scranton, Bay St. Louis, Handsboro, Pascagoula, Pass Christian, Biloxi, Moss Point, Long Beach, Ocean Springs, etc.; Also a Short Sketch of the Men Who Have Made Them Prominent*. Pass Christian, MI: Pass Christian Historical Society, 1991.

Eastern State Penitentiary. "Home." www.easternstate.org.

1880 Harrison Co., Mississippi federal census. T9_648, 8, ED 139.

Ellis, Dan. *Mississippi Gulf Coast—A Panorama of History and Culture*. Pass Christian, MS: Dan Ellis Publisher, 1998.

Eric's Gourmet Root Beer Site. "The History of Root Beer." www.gourmetrootbeer.com.

Etlin, Richard A. "Père Lachaise and the Garden Cemetery." *Journal of Garden History* 4, no. 3 (1984): 117–20.

FamilySearch. "Louisiana, Parish Marriages, 1837–1957, Edward Barq and Elodie Graugnard, 13 May 1898; citing Orleans, Louisiana, United States, various parish courthouses, Louisiana; FHL microfilm 912,049." www.ident.familysearch.org, March 12, 2018.

Federal Reserve Bank of Chicago. "The Life and Times of Nicolas Dutot." November 2009.

Find a Grave. www.findagrave.com.

Franklin, John Hope. *The Emancipation Proclamation*. Garden City, NY: Doubleday, 1963.

Gayarré, Charles. *History of Louisiana*. New York: W.J. Widdleton, 1845, 148–66.

Geman, Helyette. *Agricultural Finance: From Crops to Land, Water and Infrastructure*. Chichester, UK: John Wiley and Sons Inc., 2014.

Goodspeed Brothers. *Biographical and Historical Memoirs of Mississippi*. Vol. 2. Chicago: Goodspeed Publishing Company, 1891.

Greenwell, Dale. *Images of America: D'Iberville and St. Martin*. Charleston, SC: Arcadia Publishing, 2014.

Grisham, W.C. Commentary. *Southern Galaxy*, March 11, 1830, 4.

Guice, Julia Cook. *Marriages-Harrison County, Mississippi (1841–1899)*. Biloxi: City of Biloxi, 1968.

Harding, Thomas S. *College Literary Societies: Their Contribution to Higher Education in the United States, 1815–1876*. New York: Pageant Press International, 1971.

Hardy, Arthur. "Rex's 'Boeuf Gras' Links Carnival to Ancient Celebration." *New Orleans Advocate*, February 27, 2017.

Harrison County Census, 1860, 1870, 1880, 1900.

Harrison County, Mississippi Land Deed Book.

Harrison County, Mississippi Marriage Record Book 6.

"Historical French Documents of the Eighteenth Century; From the Archives of Jean-Frédéric Phélpeaux Compte de Maurepas." Parke-Bernet Galleries, 1962.

Hough, Emerson. *The Mississippi Bubble*. New York: McKinlay, Stone & Mackenzie, 1902.

Humphrey, Thomas M. "The Real Bills Doctrine" *Federal Reserve Bank of Richmond Economic Review 5 (1982):* 4–6.

Jackson County, Mississippi Land Deed Book.

Jefferson, Thomas. *The Works of Thomas Jefferson, Federal Edition*. Vol. 10. New York: G.P. Putnam's Sons, 1904–5.

Johnston, Norman. *Eastern State Penitentiary: Crucible of Good Intentions*. Philadelphia: Philadelphia Museum of Art, 1994.

Josephites. "Our Mission." www.josephites.org.

Kahan, Paul. *Eastern State Penitentiary: A History*. Charleston, SC: The History Press, 2008.

Kelley, Laura D. *Know LA Encyclopedia of Louisiana*. Edited by David Johnson. New Orleans: Louisiana Endowment for the Humanities, 2010, s.v. "Yellow Fever."

Landry, Jamey. "Elmer's CheeWees—the Big Cheese of New Orleans." *Inside New Orleans* 1, no. 1 (April 2015): periodical, 1–3.

Lang, John H. *History of Harrison County, Mississippi*. Gulfport, MI: Dixie Press, 1936.

Lepre, Jerome. *Catholic Church Records Diocese of Biloxi, Mississippi*. Biloxi: Diocese of Biloxi, Mississippi, 1991.

———. *The Caillavet Family*. Biloxi: Mississippi Coast History and Genealogical Society, 1984.

———. *The Delaunay Family*. New Orleans, LA.: J. Lepre, 1988.

———. *The Krohn Family*. Biloxi: Mississippi Coast History and Genealogical Society, 1989.

———. *The Seymour Family History*. Biloxi: Mississippi Coast History and Genealogical Society, 1995.

Lever, Evelyne. *Marie Antoinette: The Last Queen of France*. London: Portrait, 2010.

Levy, Jillian, CHHC. "Sarsaparilla: The Healing Herb with Many Uses, Benefits + Recipes." February 7, 2020. www.draxe.com.

Lossky, Andrew. *The Nature of Political Power According to Louis XIV*. New York: Doubleday & Company, 1967.

Louisiana Economic Development News Release. "Elmer Chocolate Announces $40 Million Manufacturing Expansion in Ponchatoula." December 30, 2014.

Manning, Thomas A. *History of Air Education and Training Command, 1942–2002*. Randolph Air Force Base, TX: Office of History and Research, Headquarters, AETC, 2005.

Margry. *Découvertes et Establissements des Français*. Paris: Maisonneuve et C. Lecclerc, 1887.

Martin, Douglas. "Eugene Marino, Black Archbishop, Dies at 66." *New York Times*, November 16, 2000.

Martin, F.X. *The History of Louisiana from the Earliest Period*. New Orleans: N.p., 1827, 325.

Mayer, Robert G. *Embalming: History, Theory & Practice*. New York: McGraw-Hill, 2000.

McWilliams, Richebourg Gaillard. *Fleur de Lys and Calumet Being the Pénicaut Narrative of French Adventure in Louisiana*. Baton Rouge: Louisiana State University Press, 1953.

Miester, Mark, and Michael DeMocker. "Robert Nelson—Elmer Candy." *Tulanian*, 2004.

Mississippi Archaeology. Biloxi, MS: Mississippi Deptartment of Archives and History and the Mississippi Archaeological Association, 1995.

Mississippi Gulf Coast Convention and Visitors Bureau.

Morrison, B.L. *Louisiana's Funeral Customs, Graves & Graveyards.* Gretna, LA: Gulf South Press, 1983.

Murphy, Antoin. *John Law: Economic Theorist and Policy-Maker.* Oxford, UK: Clarendon Press, 1997.

Murphy, Larry G., J.G. Melton and Gary L. Ward. *Encyclopedia of African American Religions*. New York: Routledge, 2011.

National Park Service. "NPS Focus." National Register of Historic Places. www.nrhp.nps.focus.gov.

New England Farmer. Boston: J. Nourse, 1849.

Nuwer, Deanne Stephens. "'The Biloxi Fishermen Are Killing the Goose that Laid the Golden Egg:' The Seafood Strike of 1932." *Journal of Mississippi History* 66, no. 4 (Winter 2004): 31–34.

Ohr-O'Keefe Museum of Art. "Pleasant Reed Interpretive Center." www.georgeohr.org.

O'Neill, Charles E., and Marcel Giraud. "A History of French Louisiana: An Essay Review of a History of French Louisiana. Volume One. The Reign of Louis XIV, 1698–1715." *Louisiana Historical Association* 16, no. 3 (Summer 1975): 1–10.

Over Caffeinated. "Caffeine and Ingredients in Barq's Root Beer." Caffeine Database. www.overcaffeinated.org.

Ownby, Ted, Charles Reagan Wilson and Anna Stanfield Harris. "Pleasant Reed House." In *Mississippi Encyclopedia*, 169. Jackson: University Press of Mississippi, 2017.

Pascagoula Democrat-Star.

Pearce, Brian, and Marcel Giraud. *A History of French Louisiana: The Company of the Indies, 1723–1731.* Baton Rouge: Louisiana State University Press, 1991.

Perez, Mary. "The Hermit of Deer Island Was Keeping a Secret. A Researcher Just Revealed What It Was." *Sun-Herald*, October 19, 2017.

———. "The Infamous Hermit of Deer Island 'Lied About His Life,' Historian Says." *Sun-Herald*, February 20, 2013.

Phelps. *Louisiana*. N.p.: Nabu Press, 2010.

Pierre Quave Store Journal, 1857–62. Archives of the Biloxi Public Library.

Pintado Papers. Mobile County Historical Library, Mobile, Alabama.

Pollack, Peter. *The Picture History of Photography*. New York: Harry N. Abrams Inc., 1969.

Posey, Zoe. "Gulf Coast Reminiscences of Jas. A. Cuevas of Days Before Sixties." *Times Picayune*, May 7, 1922.

Powell, Murella Hebert. *"Skeet": The Public Life of Walter Henry Hunt—American*. Biloxi, MI: M.H. Powell, 1988.

"Rago, David (appraiser, Dallas, Texas)." *Antiques Roadshow*. Aired on the Public Broadcasting System on June 28, 2008.

Riccards, Michael P. "Reid, Whitelaw." *American National Biography Online*. February 2000. www.anb.org.

Roberts, Deering J. *Southern Practitioner: February 1902* (classic reprint). N.p.: Forgotten Books, 2016, 38.

Robinson, Charles M., III, ed. *The Diaries of John Gregory Bourke*. Vol. 2. Denton: University of North Texas Press, 2005.

Rowland, Dunbar. *Official and Statistical Register of the State of Mississippi*. Salem, MA: Higginson Book Co., 1917.

Rowland, Dunbar, and H. Grady Howell. *Military History of Mississippi, 1803–1898*. Spartanburg, SC: Reprint Co., 1988.

Runkle, Benjamin Piatt. *Sigma Chi Quarterly* 16, no. 4 (July 1896): 1–2.

Schexnayder, Jessica H., and Mary H. Manhein. *Fragile Grounds: Louisiana's Endangered Cemeteries*. Jackson: University Press of Mississippi, 2017.

Sigma Chi Fraternity. "History of Sigma Chi." www.olemiss.edu.

———. "The Founding of Sigma Chi." www.ilwwcm.sigmachi.org.

St. Louis Cathedral, New Orleans, Louisiana. Marriage book 3 (1806–1821), 2,246 A 818.

Sullivan, Charles L., and Murella Hebert Powell. *The Mississippi Gulf Coast—Portrait of a People*. Sun Valley, CA: American Historical Press, 1999.

Sun Herald. "Eugene Marino, 1st Black Catholic Archbishop, Dies of Heart Attack in Atlanta." December 4, 2000.

Sun Herald, March 4, 1997.

United States Army Center of Military History. "Indian Wars Period Medal of Honor Recipients." Medal of Honor Citations. www.history.army.mil, January 27, 2009.

———. "Special Unit Designations." April 21, 2010. www.history.army.mil.

United States Coast Guard. "Lighthouses: Then and Now." www.uscg.mil.

United States Geological Survey. "Black Hills." Geographic Names Information System. www.usgs.gov.

U.S. Census Bureau. "U.S. Census, 1850; family 340; census place: Jackson County, Mississippi; roll M432_374; page 23A; image 51." www.census.gov.

U.S. Statute 19, 254. Enacted on February 28, 1877.

Warner, Ezra. *Generals in Gray: Lives of the Confederate Commanders.* Baton Rouge: Louisiana State University Press, 1959.

Wheeler, Major General Joseph, Colonel Charles E. Hooker, Charles E. Wheeler and Brigadier General Clement A. Evans, eds. *Confederate Military History*. Vol. 12. Atlanta: Confederate Publishing, 1899.

Williams, Tate. "In the Garden Cemetery: The Revival of America's First Urban Parks." *American Forests,* Spring/Summer 2014. www.americanforests.org.

ABOUT THE AUTHOR

John Cuevas was born and raised in Gulfport, Mississippi, and has been researching coastal history since the 1950s. His family is one of the oldest pioneer families between Mobile and New Orleans. As the creative director of his own advertising firm in Atlanta for more than twenty-five years, he worked with some of the nation's top companies, winning gold awards in radio, television and print advertising. Cuevas has written articles and books about the Mississippi Gulf Coast. His book *Cat Island* (McFarland, 2011) is considered to be the definitive history of that Gulf Coast barrier island. His book *Discovering Cat Island: Photographs and History* (University Press of Mississippi, 2018) is a coffee table photographic guide to the historic sites of the island. He has recently published two books on the history of Gulfport, Mississippi. *Lost Gulfport* (Arcadia Publishing, 2018) gives a walking tour of downtown in the 1950s and 1960s, before Hurricanes Camille and Katrina destroyed the business district. *Growing Up in Gulfport* (The History Press, 2019) is a highlight of the popular culture of the 1950s and 1960s on the Gulf Coast, featuring the local bands, the advent of rock 'n' roll, the way we dressed, the styles of our homes and cars and the transition from radio programs to television.